HOUSING ISSUES, LAWS AND PROGRAMS

THE LOW-INCOME HOUSING TAX CREDIT

ELEMENTS AND OVERSIGHT ISSUES

HOUSING ISSUES, LAWS AND PROGRAMS

Additional books in this series can be found on Nova's website under the Series tab.

Additional e-books in this series can be found on Nova's website under the e-book tab.

HOUSING ISSUES, LAWS AND PROGRAMS

THE LOW-INCOME HOUSING TAX CREDIT

ELEMENTS AND OVERSIGHT ISSUES

YVETTE DANIELS
EDITOR

New York

Library of Congress Cataloging-in-Publication Data

ISBN: 978-1-63484-569-4

Published by Nova Science Publishers, Inc. † New York

CONTENTS

PREFACE

The low-income housing tax credit (LIHTC) program is one of the federal government's primary policy tools for encouraging the development and rehabilitation of affordable rental housing. These non-refundable federal housing tax credits are awarded to developers of qualified rental projects via a competitive application process administered by state housing finance authorities. Developers typically sell their tax credits to outside investors in exchange for equity. Selling the tax credits reduces the debt developers would otherwise have to incur and the equity they would otherwise have to contribute. With lower financing costs, tax credit properties can potentially offer lower, more affordable rents. The LIHTC is estimated to cost the government an average of approximately $7 billion annually. This book discusses LIHTC's fixed subsidy and variable rates; addresses the Internal Revenue Service's oversight of LIHTC; and how LIHTC administration and oversight compare with that of other tax credit programs.

In: The Low-Income Housing Tax Credit ISBN: 978-1-63484-569-4
Editor: Yvette Daniels

Chapter 1

AN INTRODUCTION TO THE LOW-INCOME HOUSING TAX CREDIT*

Mark P. Keightley and Jeffrey M. Stupak

SUMMARY

The low-income housing tax credit (LIHTC) program is one of the federal government's primary policy tools for encouraging the development and rehabilitation of affordable rental housing. These non-refundable federal housing tax credits are awarded to developers of qualified rental projects via a competitive application process administered by state housing finance authorities. Developers typically sell their tax credits to outside investors in exchange for equity. Selling the tax credits reduces the debt developers would otherwise have to incur and the equity they would otherwise have to contribute. With lower financing costs, tax credit properties can potentially offer lower, more affordable rents. The LIHTC is estimated to cost the government an average of approximately $7 billion annually.

The LIHTC program was originally designed to provide a 30% subsidy for rehabilitated rental housing via the so-called 4% credit, and a 70% subsidy for newly constructed rental housing via the so-called 9% credit. To ensure that the 30% or 70% subsidies were achieved, the U.S. Department of the Treasury designed a formula for determining the

---

* This is an edited, reformatted and augmented version of a Congressional Research Service publication RS22389, prepared for Members and Committees of Congress, dated July 21, 2015.

effective 4% and 9% LIHTC rates. The formula depends in part on current market interest rates that fluctuate over time. These fluctuations have caused the LIHTC rates to change over time, and typically have resulted in effective LIHTCs below the 4% and 9% thresholds. Developers and investors have expressed concern over the uncertainty that the variable LIHTC rate changes introduce into the program.

The Housing and Economic Recovery Act of 2008 (P.L. 110-289) temporarily changed the credit rate formula used for new construction. The act effectively placed a floor equal to 9% on the new construction tax credit rate. The 9% credit rate floor originally only applied to new construction placed in service before December 31, 2013. The 4% tax credit rate that is applied to rehabilitation construction or new construction jointly financed with tax-exempt bonds remained unaltered by the act. Most recently, the Tax Increase Prevention Act of 2014 (P.L. 113-295) extended the 9% credit floor for one year, which the Joint Committee on Taxation (JCT) estimated would result in a10-year revenue loss of less than $500,000. In the 114th Congress, H.R. 1142 and S. 1193 would permanently extend the 9% floor and introduce a permanent floor for the 4% credit.

On December 10, 2014, House Ways and Means Committee Chairman Dave Camp introduced the Tax Reform Act of 2014 (H.R. 1), which proposed several changes to the LIHTC program. The most significant change involved the method for distributing credits to developers. When H.R. 1 was introduced, each state was given an authorized credit amount equal to $2.30 per resident, with a minimum authority of $2,635,000 for low-population states. State and local housing finance authorities (HFAs) then allocate the credits to developers to offset a project's qualified basis (certain eligible costs). Under the reform proposal, HFAs would allocate *qualified basis* not *credits* to developers. Allocation authority for each state would be limited to $31.20 per person, with a minimum authority of $36,300,000. The reform also proposed repealing the so-called 4% credit, eliminating enhanced financing for certain high-cost areas, extending the credit period from 10 years to 15 years, and eliminating the national pool of unused LIHTCs, along with several other smaller changes. The 10-year revenue gain associated with this provision was estimated to be $10.4 billion.

OVERVIEW

The low-income housing tax credit (LIHTC) was created by the Tax Reform Act of 1986 (P.L. 99- 514) to provide an incentive for the development and rehabilitation of affordable rental housing. These federal housing tax credits are awarded to developers of qualified projects via a competitive application process administered by state housing finance authorities (HFAs). Developers either use the credits or sell them to investors to raise capital for real estate projects, which, in turn, reduces the debt or equity contribution that would otherwise be required of developers. With lower financing costs, tax credit properties can potentially expand the supply of affordable rental housing. The LIHTC is estimated to cost the government an average of nearly $7 billion annually.[1]

Two types of LIHTCs are available depending on the nature of the rental housing construction. The so-called 9% credit is generally reserved for new construction. Each year for 10 years a tax credit equal to roughly 9% of a project's qualified basis (cost of construction) may be claimed. The applicable credit rate is not actually 9%; instead, the specific rate that a project will receive is set so that the present value of the 10-year stream of credits equals 70% of a project's qualified basis.[2] The formula used to ensure the 70% subsidy is achieved depends in part on current market interest rates that fluctuate over time.[3] These fluctuations have also caused the LIHTC rate to change over time. When interest rates are relatively low, the 70% subsidy can be achieved with a lower credit rate than when interest rates are relatively high. Since 1986, the 9% credit has ranged between 7.35% and 9.27%.[4]

The so-called 4% credit is typically claimed for rehabilitated housing and new construction that is financed with tax-exempt bonds.[5] Like the 9% credit, the 4% credit is claimed annually over a 10- year credit period. The actual credit rate fluctuates around 4%, but is set by the Treasury to deliver a subsidy equal to 30% of a project's qualified basis in present value terms. At one point, the 4% credit rate had fallen to as low as 3.15%.[6] For both the 4% and 9% credit it is the subsidy levels (30% or 70%) that are explicitly specified in the Internal Revenue Code (IRC), not the credit rates.

To understand the mechanics of the LIHTC, consider a new affordable housing apartment complex with a qualified basis of $1 million. Since the project involves new construction it will qualify for the 9% credit and generate a stream of tax credits equal to $90,000 (9% × $1 million) per year for 10 years, or $900,000 in total. Under the appropriate interest rate the present value of the $900,000 stream of tax credits should be equal to $700,000, resulting in a 70% subsidy. The situation would be similar if the project involved rehabilitated construction except the developer would be entitled to a stream of tax credits equal to $40,000 (4% × $1 million) per year for 10 years, or $400,000 in total. The present value of the $400,000 stream of tax credits should be equal to $300,000, resulting in a 30% subsidy.

THE ALLOCATION PROCESS

The process of allocating, awarding, and then claiming the LIHTC is complex and lengthy. The process begins at the federal level with each state receiving an annual LIHTC allocation in accordance with federal law. State housing agencies then allocate credits to developers of rental housing according to federally required, but state created, allocation plans. The process typically ends with developers selling allocated credits to outside investors in exchange for equity. A more detailed discussion of each level of the allocation process is presented below.

Federal Allocation to States

LIHTCs are first allocated to each state according to its population. In 2015, states received a LIHTC allocation of $2.30 per person, with a minimum small population state allocation of $2,680,000.[7] The state allocation limits do not apply to the 4% credits which are automatically packaged with tax-exempt bond financed projects.[8] The administration of the tax credit program is typically carried out by each state's Housing Finance Agency (HFA).

State Allocation to Developers

State HFAs allocate credits to developers of rental housing according to federally required, but state created, Qualified Allocation Plans (QAPs). Federal law requires that the QAP give priority to projects that serve the lowest income households and that remain affordable for the longest period of time. Many states have two allocation periods per year. Developers apply for the credits by proposing plans to state agencies. Types of developers include nonprofit organizations, for-profit organizations, joint ventures, partnerships, limited partnerships, trusts, corporations, and limited liability corporations.

An allocation to a developer does not imply that all allocated tax credits will be claimed. An allocation simply means tax credits are set aside for a developer. Once a developer receives an allocation it has several years to complete its project. Credits may not be claimed until a project is completed and occupied, also known as "placed in service." Tax credits that are not allocated by states are added to a national pool and then redistributed to states that apply for the excess credits. To be eligible for an excess credit allocation, a state must have allocated its entire previous allotment of tax credits. This use or lose feature gives states an incentive to allocate all of their tax credits to developers.

In order to be eligible for a LIHTC allocation, properties are required to meet certain tests that restrict both the amount of rent that is assessed to tenants and the income of eligible tenants. The "income test" for a qualified low-income housing project requires that the project owner irrevocably elect one of two income level tests, either a 20-50 test or a 40-60 test. In order to satisfy the first test, at least 20% of the units must be occupied by individuals with income of 50% or less of the area's median gross income, adjusted for family size. To satisfy the second test, at least 40% of the units must be occupied by individuals with income of 60% or less of the area's median gross income, adjusted for family size.[9] A qualified low-income housing project must also meet the "gross rents test" by ensuring rents do not exceed 30% of the elected 50% or 60% of area median gross income, depending on which income test the project elected.[10]

The types of projects eligible for the LIHTC are apartment buildings, single family dwellings, duplexes, and townhouses. Projects may include more than one building. Tax credit project types also vary by the type of tenants served. Housing can be for families or special needs populations including the elderly.

Enhanced LIHTCs are available for difficult development areas (DDAs) and qualified census tracts (QCTs) as an incentive to developers to invest in more distressed areas: areas where the need is greatest for affordable housing, but which can be the most difficult to develop.[11] In these distressed areas, the LIHTC can be claimed for 130% (instead of the normal 100%) of the project's total cost excluding land costs. This also means that available credits can be increased by up to 30%. HERA (P.L. 110-289) enacted changes that allow an HFA to classify any building it sees fit as difficult to develop and hence, eligible for the enhanced credit.

Developers and Investors

Upon receipt of a LIHTC allocation, developers typically exchange the tax credits for equity. For-profit developers can either retain tax credits as financing for projects or sell them to investors; nonprofit developers sell tax credits. Taxpayers claiming the tax credits are usually investors, not developers. The tax credits cannot be claimed until the real estate development is complete and operable. This means that more than a year or two could pass between the time of the tax credit allocation and the time the credit is claimed. If, for example, a project were completed in July of 2015, depending on the filing period of the investor, the tax credits may not begin to be claimed until sometime in 2015.

Trading tax credits, or selling them, refer to the process of exchanging tax credits for equity investment in real estate projects. Developers recruit investors to provide equity to fund development projects and offer the tax credits to those investors in exchange for their commitment. When credits are sold, the sale is usually structured with a limited partnership between the developer and the investor, and sometimes administered by syndicators who must adhere to the complex provisions of the tax code.[12] As the general partner, the developer has a very small ownership percentage but maintains the authority to build and run the project on a day-to-day basis. The investor, as a limited partner, has a large ownership percentage with an otherwise passive role. Syndicators charge a fee for overseeing the investment transactions.

Typically, investors do not expect the project to produce income. Instead, investors look to the credits, which will be used to offset their income tax liabilities, as their return on investment. The return investors receive is determined in part by the market price of the tax credits. The market price of tax credits fluctuates, but in normal economic conditions the price typically ranges from the mid-$0.80s to low-$0.90s per $1.00 tax credit. The larger the difference between the market price of the credits and their face value ($1.00), the larger the return to investors. The investor can also receive tax benefits related to any tax losses generated through the project's operating costs, interest on its debt, and deductions such as depreciation.

The type of tax credit investor has changed over the life of the LIHTC. Upon the introduction of the LIHTC in 1986, public partnerships were the primary source of equity investment in tax credit projects, but diminished profit margins have driven some syndicators out of the retail investment market. Although there are individual tax credit investors, in recent years, the vast majority of investors have come from corporations, either investing directly or through private partnerships.[13]

Different types of investors have different motivations for investing in tax credits. Some investors are motivated by the Community Reinvestment Act (CRA), which considers LIHTC investments favorably.[14] Other investors include real estate, insurance, utility, and manufacturing firms, many of which list the rate of return on investment as their primary purpose for investing in tax credits. Tax sheltering is the second-most highly ranked purpose for investing.[15]

The LIHTC finances part of the total cost of many projects rather than the full cost and, as a result, must be combined with other resources. The financial resources that may be used in conjunction with the LIHTC include conventional mortgage loans provided by private lenders and alternative financing and grants from public or private sources. Individual states provide financing as well, some of which may be in the form of state tax credits modeled after the federal provision. Additionally, some LIHTC projects may have tenants who receive other government subsidies such as housing vouchers.

RECENT LEGISLATIVE DEVELOPMENTS

The Housing and Economic Recovery Act of 2008 (P.L. 110-289) temporarily changed the credit rate formula used for new construction. The act effectively placed a floor equal to 9% on the new construction tax credit rate. The 9% credit rate floor originally only applied to new construction placed in service before December 31, 2013. The 4% tax credit rate that is applied to rehabilitation construction or new construction jointly financed with tax-exempt bonds remained unaltered by the act. Most recently, the Tax Increase Prevention Act of 2014 (P.L. 113-295) extended the 9% credit floor for one year, which the Joint Committee on Taxation (JCT) estimated would result in a10-year revenue loss of less than $500,000. In the 114th Congress, H.R. 1142 and S. 1193 would permanently extend the 9% floor and introduce a permanent floor for the 4% credit.

On December 10, 2014, House Ways and Means Committee Chairman Dave Camp introduced the Tax Reform Act of 2014 (H.R. 1), which proposed several changes to the LIHTC program. The most significant change involved the method for distributing credits to developers. At the time, each state was given an authorized credit amount equal to $2.30 per resident, with a small state minimum authority of $2,635,000. State and local housing finance authorities (HFAs) then allocate the credits to developers to offset a project's qualified basis (certain eligible costs). Under the reform proposal, HFAs would allocate *qualified basis* not *credits* to developers. Allocation authority for each state would have been limited to $31.20 per person, with a minimum small state authority of $36,300,000. The reform also proposed repealing the so-called 4% credit, eliminating enhanced financing for certain high-cost areas, extending the credit period from 10 years to 15 years, and eliminating the national pool of unused LIHTCs, along with several other smaller changes.

The JCT estimated the 10-year revenue gain associated with this provision to be $10.4 billion.[16]

End Notes

[1] U.S. Congress, Joint Committee on Taxation, Estimates of Federal Tax Expenditures for Fiscal Years 2014-2018, committee print, 113th Cong., 2nd sess., August 5, 2014, JCX-97-14.

[2] The concept of present value is used when it is necessary to value a stream of money that is expected to be received over time. Because of the ability to earn a return on money received sooner rather than later, money received in the future is less valuable than money received today. The present value concept accounts for this "time value of money" by discounting money expected to be received at different points in time. Usually, discounting is carried out using an interest rate because interest rates measure the time value of money.

[3] See CRS Report RS22917, The Low-Income Housing Tax Credit Program: The Fixed Subsidy and Variable Rate, by Mark P. Keightley and Jeffrey M. Stupak for a detailed discussion of how the LIHTC rates are calculated.

[4] The lower bound of this range is the rate that would have prevailed in absence of the 9% credit floor. U.S. Department of the Treasury, Internal Revenue Service, Revenue Ruling 2012-24, Table 4, Appropriate Percentages Under Section 42(b)(2) for September 2012, Internal Revenue Bulletin 2012-36, September 4, 2012, and Novogradac & Company LLP, "Appendix H: List of Monthly Credit Percentages," in Low-Income Housing Tax Credit Handbook, 2006 ed. (2006), p. 845.

[5] A developer using federal tax-exempt bonds can qualify for the 9% credit if they reduce the project's eligible basis by the amount of the tax-exempt bond subsidy.

[6] U.S. Department of the Treasury, Internal Revenue Service, Revenue Ruling 2012-24, Table 4, Appropriate Percentages Under Section 42(b)(2) for September 2012, Internal Revenue Bulletin 2012-36, September 4, 2012.

[7] From 1986 through 2000, the initial credit allocation amount was $1.25 per capita. The allocation was increased to $1.50 in 2001, to $1.75 in 2002 and 2003, and indexed for inflation annually thereafter. The initial minimum tax credit ceiling for small states was $2,000,000, and was indexed for inflation annually after 2003.

[8] Tax-exempt bonds are issued subject to a private activity bond volume limit per state. For more information, see CRS Report RL31457, Private Activity Bonds: An Introduction, by Steven Maguire.

[9] Internal Revenue Code (IRC) §42(g)(1).

[10] IRC §42(g)(2).

[11] IRC §42(d)(5).

[12] Syndicators are intermediaries who exist almost exclusively to administer tax credit deals. In the early years of the LIHTC, syndicators were more prevalent. In later years, as the number of corporate investors in the LIHTC grew and interacted directly with developers, the role of syndicators diminished.

[13] HousingFinance.com, "Corporate Investment and the Future of Tax Credits: What Should You Expect," at http://www.housingfinance.com/housingreferencecenter/Corporate_ Investment. html, June 19, 2008.

[14] In 2005, an estimated 43% of LIHTC investors were subject to the CRA. U.S. Department of the Treasury. Office of the Comptroller of the Currency, Low Income Housing Tax Credits:

Fact Sheet August 2005, pp. 1-2, at http://www.occ.treas.gov/Cdd/fact%20sheet%20LIHTC.pdf, June 19, 2008.

[15] Jean L. Cummings and Denise DiPasquale, "Building Affordable Housing: An Analysis of the Low-Income Housing Tax Credit," City Research, 1998, p. 33.

[16] U.S. Congress, Joint Committee on Taxation, Estimated Revenue Effects of the "Tax Reform Act of 2014," 113th Cong., 2nd sess., February 26, 2014, JCX-20-14 (Washington: GPO, 2014).

In: The Low-Income Housing Tax Credit
Editor: Yvette Daniels
ISBN: 978-1-63484-569-4

Chapter 2

THE LOW-INCOME HOUSING TAX CREDIT PROGRAM: THE FIXED SUBSIDY AND VARIABLE RATE*

Mark P. Keightley and Jeffrey M. Stupak

SUMMARY

The Low-Income Housing Tax Credit (LIHTC) program was originally designed to provide financing for rehabilitated and newly constructed rental housing with a subsidy equal to 30% and 70% of construction costs, respectively. To ensure that the 30% or 70% subsidies were achieved, the U.S. Department of the Treasury designed a formula for determining the LIHTC rate. The LIHTC rate is a percentage of the initial qualified investment in a low-income housing project. A higher LIHTC rate generates a larger tax credit. The formula used to determine the rate depends in part on current market interest rates that fluctuate over time. These fluctuations have also caused the LIHTC rate to change over time. Developers and investors have expressed concern over the uncertainty that the variable LIHTC rate changes introduce into the program.

The Housing and Economic Recovery Act of 2008, P.L. 110-289, temporarily changed the credit rate formula used for new construction.

* This is an edited, reformatted and augmented version of a Congressional Research Service publication RS22917, prepared for Members and Committees of Congress, dated September 1, 2015.

The act effectively placed a floor equal to 9% on the new construction LIHTC rate. The 9% credit rate floor originally only applied to new construction placed in service before December 31, 2013. The tax credit rate (known as the 4% credit) that is applied to rehabilitation construction remained unaltered by the act. The American Taxpayer Relief Act of 2012 (P.L. 112-240) extended the 9% floor for credit allocations made before January 1, 2014. Most recently, the Tax Increase Prevention Act of 2014 (P.L. 113-295) retroactively extended the 9% floor through the end of 2014.

This report explains the original method for determining the LIHTC rate, the relationship between interest rates and the LIHTC rate, the temporary 9% tax credit rate floor instituted by P.L. 110-289 and extended by P.L. 112- 240 and P.L. 113-295, and recent proposals to extend the floor again. Historical data on the credit rates are also analyzed in order to gain insight into the potential effect of the LIHTC rate floors.

INTRODUCTION

The low-income tax credit (LIHTC), created under the Tax Reform Act of 1986, P.L. 99-514, is a federally provided tax incentive that is intended to encourage the development of affordable rental housing for low-income families. LIHTCs are allocated to each state according to its population. States, in turn, award LIHTCs to developers of qualified projects. Developers can either keep the tax credits to reduce their own tax liability, or sell them to investors to raise capital for their projects. The LIHTC, which is claimed annually over a 10-year period, is used to offset a portion of the project's cost. The cost offset provides developers of affordable rental housing a production subsidy, and, as a result, the tax credit can potentially lead to the construction of more affordable rental properties.

THE ORIGINAL LIHTC RATE FORMULA

Two types of LIHTCs are available depending on the nature of the rental housing project. The so-called 9% credit is designed to deliver a 70% subsidy to new rental construction, while the 4% credit is designed to deliver a 30% subsidy to rehabilitated housing and new construction that is financed with tax-exempt bonds.[1] For the purposes of the program, the subsidy is the present value of the 10-year tax credit stream expressed as a fraction of the project's eligible basis (costs). It is the subsidy levels (30% or 70%) that are explicitly specified in the Internal Revenue Code (IRC), not the credit rates.[2] The credit rates are to be set such that the subsidy levels specified in statute are delivered.

It is important to distinguish between a project's eligible basis and its total cost of development. Only the costs that are included in a project's eligible basis can be offset with tax credits. Eligible basis, however, excludes a number of important costs, particularly the cost of land, which can be significant. Thus, while the credit subsidizes a project's eligible basis up to 70%, the credit does not provide a 70% subsidy for the total cost of development.

To ensure that the 30% or 70% subsidies are achieved, the U.S. Department of the Treasury uses a formula for determining the LIHTC rate. The formula depends on three factors: the credit period length, the desired subsidy level, and the current interest rate. The credit period length and the subsidy levels are fixed in the formula by law, while the interest rate changes over time according to current market conditions. Given the current interest rate, the formula determines the LIHTC rate that delivers the desired subsidy level.[3] Because two different subsidy levels are possible, the formula produces two different tax credit rates—the 4% credit to ensure the 30% rehabilitation subsidy, and the 9% credit to ensure the 70% subsidy for new construction. Once the credit rate has been determined, it is multiplied by the project's eligible basis to obtain the annual amount of LIHTCs a project will receive.

Historically, the rehabilitation and new construction tax credit rates have not been exactly 4% and 9%, respectively.[4] The applicable credit rates depend on the Treasury's formula, which, in turn, depends on monthly interest rates. Since interest rates can change from month to month, so too can the LIHTC rates.[5] For example, since 1987, the tax credit rate that has delivered the 30% rehabilitation construction subsidy has approximated 4%, although it has fallen as low as 3.15%.[6] At the same time, the tax credit rate implied by the 70% new construction subsidy has roughly approximated 9%, but has fluctuated between 7.35% and 9.27%.[7] While the tax credit rates have fluctuated over time, the project subsidies themselves have remained constant at 30% and 70%.

The month-to-month fluctuation in credit rates, when combined with when the rates are actually determined, can result in developers and investors being awarded an amount of credits that is different than what they initially expected. Developers must begin arranging financing with investors early in the planning phase of a project, which requires that an expectation be made early in the planning phase about the amount of credits a project will generate. At the latest, however, tax credits may not be awarded until a project is placed in service (completed and occupied), which may be well over a year after the planning phase. This creates some uncertainty for those involved in the project.

There is also a potential issue with the method used by Treasury to ensure that the 30% and 70% subsidies are achieved; particularly, that the method may be overstating the subsidy that the LIHTC delivers. Treasury is required (by law) to use interest rates that are tied to the federal government's cost of borrowing when computing the present value of the stream of tax credits. Since U.S. government bonds are generally viewed as (practically) risk free, the interest rate they carry is generally below private market interest rates. But LIHTC projects are not risk free. Therefore, it may be more appropriate to compute the LIHTC subsidy based on a higher interest rate that reflects the riskiness of these developments. Doing so would likely produce a subsidy estimate below the 30% and 70% thresholds, unless the credit rate was increased to compensate for the use of a higher interest rate.

AN EXAMPLE

An example may be useful for understanding the original LIHTC rate formula, the relationship between the tax credit rate and the current interest rate, and the fixed project subsidy. Let us assume a newly constructed rental housing property with an eligible basis equal to $500,000. Because the project is new construction, it is eligible to receive the "9%" tax credit. As previously mentioned, the actual tax credit rate awarded will not be exactly 9%, but rather set such that the project receives a subsidy equal to 70% of the project's cost, or $350,000. The tax credit rate that satisfies this requirement will depend on the interest rate used in the Treasury's formula.

Table 1. LIHTC Rate Response to Interest Rate Change

	A	B	C
Eligible Basis (New Construction)	$500,000	$500,000	$500,000
Current Interest Rate	1.90%	2.90%	3.90%
Tax Credit Rate	7.60%	7.93%	8.26%
Credit Per Year (Cost X Credit Rate)	$38,035	$39,668	$41,322
Total Credit (Credit Per Year X 10)	$380,350	$396,680	$413,220
Present Value of Credit Stream	$350,000	$350,000	$350,000
Effective Subsidy (PV/Total Costs)	70%	70%	70%

Source: Author's calculations (assumes 100% of building units are LIHTC).

To show the dependence of the tax credit rate on the current interest rate, *Table 1* presents three different interest rate scenarios. The middle column (B) assumes an interest rate of 2.90%. Given this interest rate and the fixed 10-year credit period, the LIHTC rate formula dictates a 7.93% tax credit rate. At this credit rate, the project generates $39,668 in tax credits per year, or $396,680 in total tax credits over 10 years. The present value of the tax credits, by design of the formula, equates to 70% of the project's eligible basis, or $350,000.

Columns A and C of *Table 1* illustrate the relationship between the tax credit rate and the interest rate implied by the Treasury's original formula by considering a one percentage point deviation from the interest rate in column B. A decrease in the interest rate leads to a fall in the tax credit rate, whereas an increase in the interest rate causes the tax credit rate to rise. The subsidy, however, is constant at 70% of the project's eligible basis across both of these interest rate changes.[8]

The relationship between the interest rate, the tax credit rate, and the subsidy follows from the original design of the formula used by the Treasury to fix the present value of the subsidy. To see this, consider an increase in the interest rate. Specifically, with no tax credit rate change, an increase in the interest rate would cause the present value of the tax credit subsidy to fall below 70%. As originally enacted, however, the law required that the present value remain constant.[9] Thus, the tax credit rate increased to keep the present value of the total 10-year tax credit stream at 70%. Likewise, all else equal, a decrease in the interest rate would cause the present value of the tax credit subsidy to rise above 70%. Again, the original tax law prohibited this outcome. Therefore the tax credit rate declined in response to an interest rate decrease in order for the subsidy to be held constant.

LEGISLATIVE CHANGES AND THE 9% FLOOR

The Housing and Economic Recovery Act of 2008 (HERA, P.L. 110-289) temporarily changed the LIHTC rate to be no less than 9% for new construction placed in service before December 31, 2013. The American Taxpayer Relief Act of 2012 (P.L. 112-240) extended the 9% floor for credit allocations made before January 1, 2014. Most recently, the Tax Increase Prevention Act of 2014 (P.L. 113-295) extended the floor through the end of 2014. The change enacted by HERA and extended by P.L. 112-240 and P.L. 113-295 implied that the applicable tax credit rate for new construction was temporarily the greater of 9% or the rate as determined under the original method described above. In the 114th Congress, H.R. 1142 and S. 1193 would permanently extend the 9% floor and introduce a permanent floor for the 4% credit, while S. 1946 would only extend the 9% for any credit allocations made through the end of 2016.

The effect of the 9% tax credit rate floor (or 4% floor) depends on the spread between the original variable credit rate and the credit rate floor (see *Figure 1*). The credit rate floor has no effect if the variable credit rate is greater than the 9% floor. This is because the credit rate floor only imposes a lower bound below which the credit rate cannot fall. If the variable rate is above the floor, then the variable rate is used to determine the credits a LIHTC project will receive. In this scenario, the value of the subsidy remains at 70% of eligible basis.

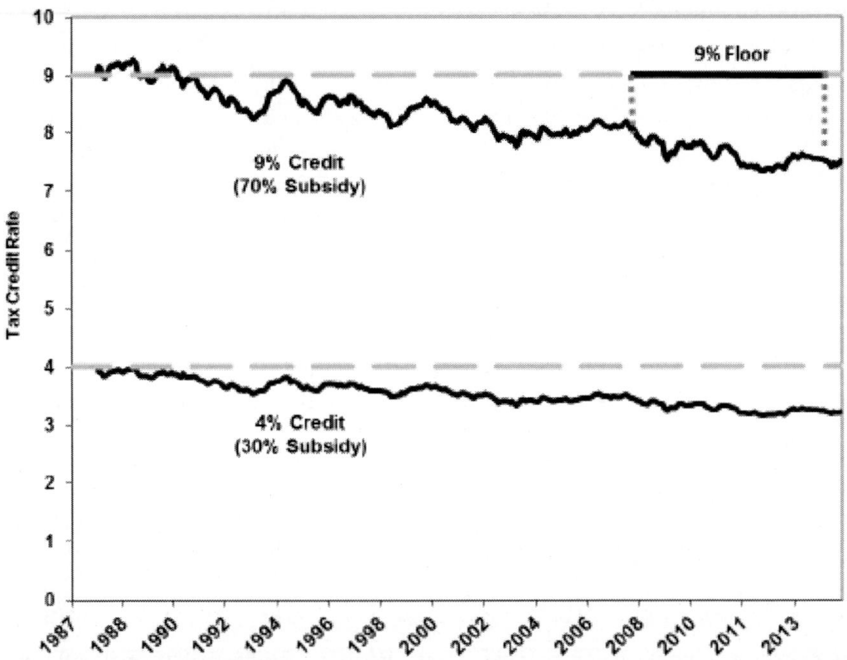

Source: CRS analysis of data from Novogradac & Company LLP, Affordable Housing Resource Center, Tax Credit Percentages, http://www.novoco.com/low_income_housing/facts_figures, visited on July 16, 2015.

Figure 1. Historical LIHTC Rates.

If, however, the variable credit rate is below the floor, then the credit rate increases to 9%. As a result, new construction projects will receive a subsidy above the 70% of eligible basis, with the subsidy increasing as the difference between the variable credit rate and the 9% floor increases. This had been the case while the 9% floor was in place, leading the effective subsidy flowing to new LIHTC construction to rise above 70%.

The increase in the subsidy resulting from the floor can be significant. For example, based on interest rates in July 2015, the 9% floor would produce a subsidy equal to 84% of a project's eligible basis.[10] Absent the floor, the subsidy, by design, would have been 70%. Thus, the floor increased the subsidy for construction by about 20% (or 14 percentage points). As mentioned previously, however, there is the issue of what is the appropriate interest rate to use when computing the LIHTC subsidy. The subsidy presented here for when the 9% floor is in place was computed using the Treasury method, which may be overstating the subsidy that is generated.

As *Figure 1* shows, there has been a recent trend downward in the 4% credit, similar to that exhibited by the 9% credit. If this trend continues then the 4% credit rate as determined under the original formula may be expected to be below the proposed floor, and the new method for determining the 4% credit would increase the value of the subsidy these projects receive to above 30%. For example, 4% credit-financed housing placed in service in July 2015 would have received a 37% subsidy had the floor been in place.[11]

APPENDIX. PRESENT VALUE OF LOW-INCOME TAX CREDIT STREAM

This example shows that the present value of the 10-year tax credit stream presented in Table 1 is constant across all three interest rate scenarios.

Thus, while the credit rate varies across the three interest rate scenarios in *Table 1*, the present value of the 10-year tax credit stream remains constant at $350,000, or 70% of the project's total cost.

$$PV\ tax\ credits = \sum_{t=1}^{10} \frac{k \times Q}{(1+r)^{t-1}}$$

Qualified costs are equal to $500,000 in the example presented in **Table 1**. The middle column of **Table 1** assumes an interest rate of 2.90% which results in a credit rate of 7.93%. Plugging these values in to the formula above gives

$$PV\ tax\ credits = \sum_{t=1}^{10} \frac{7.93\% \times \$500{,}000}{(1+2.90\%)^{t-1}}$$

$$= \frac{7.93\% \times \$500{,}000}{(1+2.90\%)^{0}} + \frac{7.93\% \times \$500{,}000}{(1+2.90\%)^{1}} + \ldots + \frac{7.93\% \times \$500{,}000}{(1+2.90\%)^{9}}$$

$$= \frac{\$39{,}668}{(1+2.90\%)^{0}} + \frac{\$39{,}668}{(1+2.90\%)^{1}} + \ldots + \frac{\$39{,}668}{(1+2.90\%)^{9}}$$

$$= \$350{,}000.$$

The scenario presented in the first column of **Table 1** differs from the middle column only in the assumed interest rate and credit rate. The interest rate and credit rate from the first column were 1.90% and 7.60%, respectively. Inserting these values into the present-value formula produces

$$PV\ tax\ credits = \sum_{t=1}^{10} \frac{7.60\% \times \$500{,}000}{(1+1.90\%)^{t-1}}$$

$$= \$350{,}000.$$

The last column assumes that the interest rate is 3.90% and that the credit rate is 8.26%. Using these rates and the present-value formula gives

$$PV\ tax\ credits = \sum_{t=1}^{10} \frac{8.26\% \times \$500{,}000}{(1+3.90\%)^{t-1}}$$

$$= \$350{,}000.$$

End Notes

[1] A developer using federal tax-exempt bonds can qualify for the 9% credit if they reduce the project's eligible basis by the amount of the tax-exempt bond subsidy. The applicable federal rates are based on Treasury security yields.

[2] IRC §42(b).

[3] The interest rate used by the Treasury Department is equal to 72% of the average of the mid-term applicable federal rate and the long-term applicable federal rate.

[4] The Tax Reform Act of 1986 specified that only buildings placed in service in 1987 were to receive exactly a 4% or 9% credit rate. Buildings placed in service after that were to receive a credit rate that delivered a 30% or 70% subsidy.

[5] The interest rate used by the Treasury Department is equal to 72% of the average of the mid-term applicable federal rate and the long-term applicable federal rate. The applicable federal rates are based on Treasury security yields.

[6] U.S. Department of the Treasury, Internal Revenue Service, Revenue Ruling 2012-21, Table 4, Appropriate Percentages Under Section 42(b)(1) for August 2012.

[7] U.S. Department of the Treasury, Internal Revenue Service, Revenue Ruling 89-65 , Table 4, Appropriate Percentages Under Section 42(b)(2) for May 1989, and Revenue Ruling 2012-24, Table 4, Appropriate Percentages Under Section 42(b)(1) for September 2012.

[8] The Appendix verifies that the subsidies in Table 1 are indeed constant across all three interest rate scenarios.

[9] Except buildings placed in service in 1987. See footnote 4.

[10] The subsidy was calculated as the present value of the 10-year stream of annual tax credits the 9% floor provides to a hypothetical project relative to the project's cost. The discount rate used was equal to 72% of the average of the midterm and long-term applicable federal rates (AFR) for July 2015 as listed in Internal Revenue Bulletin 2015-15, http://www.irs.gov/pub/irs-drop/rr-15-15.pdf. This is the same discount rate used in the Treasury's tax credit formula.

[11] The subsidy was calculated as the present value of the 10-year stream of annual tax credits the 4% floor would provide to a hypothetical project relative to the project's cost. The discount rate used was equal to 72% of the average of the mid-term and long-term applicable federal rates (AFR) for July 2015 as listed in Internal Revenue Bulletin 2015- 15, http://www.irs.gov/pub/irs-drop/rr-15-15.pdf.

In: The Low-Income Housing Tax Credit ISBN: 978-1-63484-569-4
Editor: Yvette Daniels

Chapter 2

LOW-INCOME HOUSING TAX CREDIT: JOINT IRS-HUD ADMINISTRATION COULD HELP ADDRESS WEAKNESSES IN OVERSIGHT*

United States Government Accountability Office

WHY GAO DID THIS STUDY

The LIHTC program, established under the Tax Reform Act of 1986, is the largest source of federal assistance for developing affordable rental housing and cost an estimated $8 billion in forgone revenue in 2014. LIHTC encourages private equity investment in low-income housing through tax credits. HFAs receive an annual allocation of tax credits and competitively award the credits to owners of qualified projects. GAO was asked to review the administration and oversight of the program. This report addresses, among other things, (1) IRS oversight of LIHTC and (2) how LIHTC administration and oversight compare with that of other tax credit programs. GAO reviewed regulations and guidance for monitoring HFAs and taxpayers; analyzed information on IRS audits of HFAs; reviewed selected programs that award tax credits similarly to LIHTC; and interviewed IRS, HUD, and HFA officials.

* This is an edited, reformatted and augmented version of the United States Government Accountability Office publication, GAO-15-330, dated July 2015.

WHAT GAO RECOMMENDS

Congress should consider designating HUD as a joint administrator of the program. HUD's role should include oversight responsibilities (such as regular monitoring of HFAs) to help address deficiencies GAO identified. Treasury agreed HUD could be responsible for analyzing the effectiveness of LIHTC, with IRS continuing to enforce tax law. HUD and IRS did not comment on the matter for congressional consideration. HUD supported consideration of a structure for enhanced interagency coordination. The association representing HFAs disagreed with the matter. GAO maintains that joint administration would strengthen program oversight.

WHAT GAO FOUND

Internal Revenue Service (IRS) oversight of the Low-Income Housing Tax Credit (LIHTC) program has been minimal. Specifically, since 1986 IRS conducted seven audits of 56 state housing finance agencies (HFA) on which IRS relies to administer and oversee the program. (HFAs are state-chartered authorities established to meet affordable housing needs.) Federal internal control standards call for monitoring to be performed continually in the course of normal operations and be ingrained in agency operations. Oversight of HFAs has been minimal, partly because LIHTC is viewed as a peripheral program in IRS in terms of its mission and priorities for resources and staffing. Without such reviews, IRS cannot determine the extent of noncompliance and other issues at HFAs.

IRS jointly administers other programs: the Historic Rehabilitation Tax Credit with the National Park Service and the New Markets Tax Credit with the Community Development Financial Institutions Fund in the Department of the Treasury. The federal agencies that work with IRS to oversee these programs have missions consistent with the purposes of these programs; they also conduct monitoring, report on performance, and collect data. For example, officials of both agencies told GAO that staff routinely conduct site visits and other project reviews. In these cases, IRS also is able to benefit from the other federal agencies' policy and subject-matter expertise. Likewise, the Department of Housing and Urban Development's (HUD) experience in administering affordable housing programs and working with HFAs may benefit IRS in its administration and oversight of the LIHTC program. More specifically, HUD relies on state and local housing agencies (including HFAs) to implement its programs and already has processes and procedures in place to oversee them. Although GAO and others have identified weakness in HUD's program evaluation and oversight activities, HUD has taken steps to address some of these issues and its existing processes and procedures constitute a framework on which further changes and improvement can be made. Moreover, IRS is not well positioned to oversee LIHTC. Since 1990, IRS has been on GAO's high-risk list due to significant capacity challenges and incomplete monitoring of tax law enforcement. IRS's budget has been reduced by 10 percent and enforcement program performance and staffing levels have declined since 2010.

Joint administration with HUD could better align program responsibilities with each agency's mission and more efficiently address existing oversight challenges. Under joint administration, IRS could retain responsibilities consistent with its mission (as it does in the other two tax credit programs). For example, IRS could continue to enforce taxpayer compliance. Assigning oversight responsibilities to HUD could involve additional resources for HUD. For LIHTC and the other two programs, GAO found that each used different mechanisms to fund administrative responsibilities. For instance, Historic Rehabilitation uses fees to fund its program, including oversight, while New Markets requests funding through annual appropriations. The level of resources that would be needed to perform an adequate level of oversight of HFAs is not known. An estimate of potential costs and funding options for financing enhanced federal oversight of the LIHTC program could benefit the agency involved and provide useful information to Congress.

ABBREVIATIONS

CDBG	Community Development Block Grant
CDE	Community Development Entity
CDFI	Community Development Financial Institutions
Code	Section 42 of the Internal Revenue Code
HFA	housing finance agency
HOME	HOME Investment Partnerships
HUD	Department of Housing and Urban Development
IRS	Internal Revenue Service
LIHTC	Low-Income Housing Tax Credit
NCSHA	National Council of State Housing Agencies

NPS	National Park Service
QAP	qualified allocation plan
SB/SE	Small Business/Self-Employed Division
SHPO	State Historic Preservation Officer
Section 1602	Grants to States for Low-Income Housing Projects in Lieu of Low-Income Housing Credits
TCAP	Tax Credit Assistance Program
TPS	Technical Preservation Services
Treasury	Department of the Treasury

***

July 15, 2015

The Honorable Charles E. Grassley
Chairman
Committee on the Judiciary
United States Senate

Dear Senator Grassley:

The Low-Income Housing Tax Credit (LIHTC) program, established under the Tax Reform Act of 1986, is the largest source of federal assistance for developing affordable rental housing and cost an estimated $8 billion in forgone revenue in 2014. The program encourages private-equity investment in low-income housing through tax credits and is administered by one federal agency and state agencies—the Internal Revenue Service (IRS) and state housing finance agencies (HFA). HFAs are state- chartered authorities established to meet the affordable housing needs of the residents of their states and administer a wide range of affordable housing and community development programs. Each state receives an annual allocation of LIHTCs, determined by statutory formula according to population.[1] HFAs then competitively award the tax credits to owners of qualified rental housing projects that reserve all or a portion of their units for low-income tenants.[2] Developers typically attempt to obtain funding for their projects by attracting third-party investors that are willing to contribute equity to the projects; the project investors then can claim the tax credits.

We and others have observed that severe resource constraints could affect the ability of IRS to administer its programs.[3] In a February 2015 report, we found that IRS staffing reductions and other budget issues affected the number of tax return examinations conducted.[4] For example, IRS's appropriations declined below fiscal year 2009 levels, affecting staff levels (a reduction of 9 percent since 2009) and examinations.

You asked us to review how the LIHTC program is administered and identify any oversight issues. This report (1) discusses how the LIHTC program is administered; (2) evaluates processes for overseeing the LIHTC program; and (3) compares the administration of other tax credit programs with LIHTC.

To determine how the LIHTC program is administered, we reviewed IRS regulations and guidance; documentation on the role of HFAs, investors, and syndicators in the LIHTC program; and specific monitoring requirements of other federal programs that also may be funding sources for projects with LIHTCs, such as the Home Investment Partnerships (HOME) program and the project-based Section 8 rental assistance program.[5] We interviewed the National Council of State Housing Agencies (NCSHA) and reviewed relevant documents for information to illustrate the number of LIHTC units that contain other federal funding. We chose this group because it represents HFAs and advocates for affordable housing. We also interviewed officials from IRS, Department of the Treasury (Treasury), Department of Housing and Urban Development (HUD), and two HFAs on program administration.[6]

To evaluate processes for overseeing the LIHTC program, we reviewed IRS policies and guidance including how HFAs and taxpayers are selected for review.[7] We reviewed federal internal control standards to identify key activities that help ensure that the program is addressing requirements and that appropriate actions are taken to address program risks.[8] We also reviewed strategic and annual reports of IRS, Treasury, and HUD to identify any program goals and performance measures on the LIHTC program. We analyzed information contained in IRS's Low- Income Housing Credit database from December 2005 to August 2014. We assessed the reliability of the database and determined that data reliability issues impeded our analysis, as discussed further in this report. Therefore, we limited our discussion to the type of information collected, the extent to which the information was collected, and potential analysis that could be conducted if the data were more complete and accurate. We also interviewed officials and reviewed documents at IRS, Treasury, HUD, and two HFAs on IRS processes for overseeing the program.

To compare the administration of other tax credit programs with the LIHTC program, we reviewed other tax credit programs administered by IRS to identify those most similar in purpose and structure to LIHTC. We focused on the Historic Rehabilitation Tax Credit and New Markets Tax Credit programs because both are aimed at encouraging community development and are jointly administered by IRS and another federal agency—the Department of Interior's National Park Service (NPS) and Treasury's Community Development Financial Institutions (CDFI) Fund, respectively. We reviewed prior GAO reports about each program.[9] In addition, we reviewed HUD's role in affordable housing, including its work with HFAs. We interviewed officials at the Departments of Interior and Treasury, and at the CDFI Fund on the administration of the Historic Rehabilitation Tax Credit and New Markets Tax Credit programs. Appendix I contains additional details about our scope and methodology.

We conducted this performance audit from February 2014 through July 2015 in accordance with generally accepted government auditing standards. Those standards require that we plan and perform the audit to obtain sufficient, appropriate evidence to provide a reasonable basis for our findings and conclusions based on our audit objectives. We believe that the evidence obtained provides a reasonable basis for our findings and conclusions based on our audit objectives.

BACKGROUND

The LIHTC program replaced older tax incentives, such as accelerated depreciation—that allowed taxpayers to deduct the costs of assets faster than their value actually declined—with a federal-state program in which HFAs receive LIHTC allocations of credits and award the credits to specific projects that meet requirements of Section 42 of the Internal Revenue Code (code).[10] Prior to the establishment of LIHTC, federal housing assistance generally involved subsides or grants administered by HUD to construct new affordable housing and to make rents affordable in existing rental housing.

An LIHTC project owner can develop new housing or acquire and rehabilitate existing housing. The projects can be apartments, single- family housing, single-room occupancy, or permanent and transitional housing for the homeless. The project may include units for low-income households and market-rate units. The amount of credit received is based on the number of low-income units.

The project owners—the taxpayers receiving LIHTCs—agree to set aside a certain percentage of the units with rents that are affordable to qualifying low-income households for at least 30 years. A project must reserve at least 20 percent of the available units for households earning up to 50 percent of the area's median gross income (adjusted for family size), or at least 40 percent of the units for households earning up to 60 percent of the area's median gross income (adjusted for family size). HUD and Treasury officials noted that in practice, LIHTC projects usually exceed these minimum affordability requirements by setting aside nearly all of their units for low-income households.

In return, taxpayers can earn a tax credit over a 15-year period (the compliance period) if they meet the affordability requirements, but can claim the credit over an accelerated time frame (the 10-year credit period), beginning in the year in which the property is placed in service (ready for occupancy) or, if the taxpayer chooses, the succeeding taxable year.[11] IRS can recapture (take back) some or all of the credits received by taxpayers if the taxpayers have not met the requirements during the compliance period. In addition, properties awarded credits after 1989 must comply with the affordability requirements for at least another 15 years (the extended use period) but are no longer subject to recapture after the compliance period.[12] HFAs may impose longer affordability restrictions on properties than the minimum 30-year period. The three time periods begin on the same day—the first day of the tax year in which the building is placed in service, or if taxpayers elect, the beginning of the following tax year. The allowable credit may be reduced (in part or in whole) for the tax year if taxpayers were not compliant with the code requirements. Taxpayers also may be subject to the recapture of credits claimed in prior years.

LIHTC is administered by IRS and state HFAs. To promote compliance with LIHTC program requirements, IRS is the federal entity responsible for (1) enforcing taxpayer compliance and (2) overseeing HFAs' implementation of the program. All 50 states, the District of Columbia, Puerto Rico, American Samoa, Guam, the Northern Mariana Islands, and the U.S. Virgin Islands have HFAs that receive LIHTC allocations.

HUD's role includes mandatory and voluntary data collection on the LIHTC program. More specifically, the agency has collected information on tenant characteristics, as mandated by the Housing and Economic Recovery Act of 2008.[13] In addition, since 1996, HUD has voluntarily collected LIHTC project-level data because of the importance of these credits as a source of funding for low-income housing. HUD also has a role in designating difficult development areas and qualified census tracts.[14] Figure 1 provides an overview of the LIHTC process and participants.

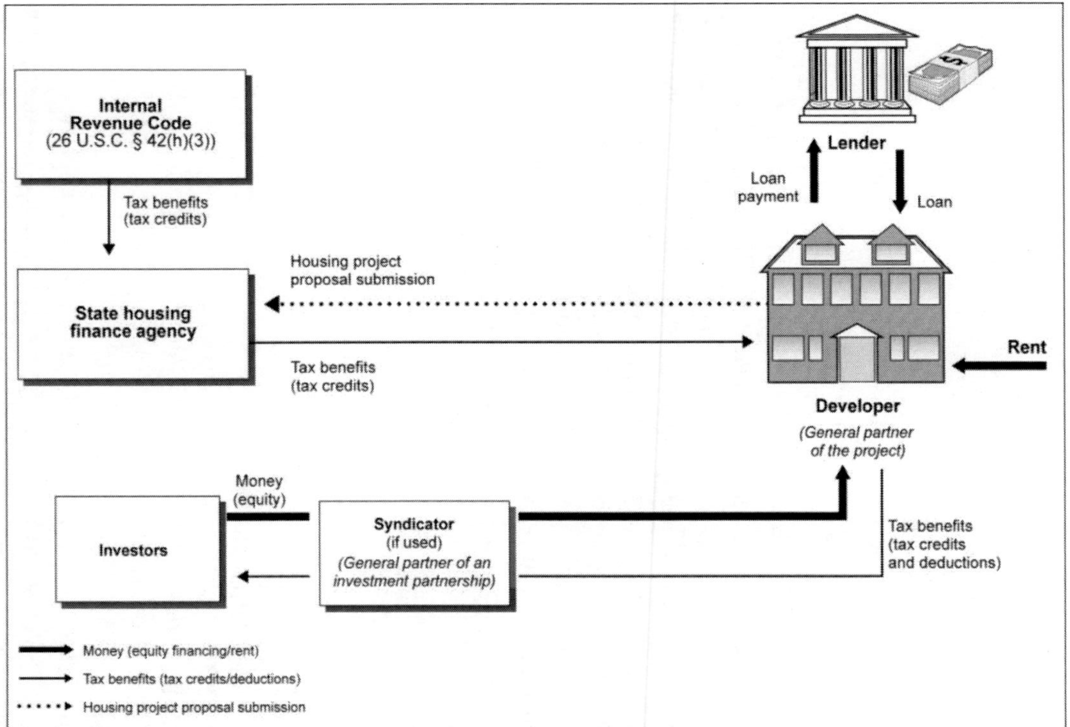

Source: GAO. | GAO-15-330

Figure 1. Overview of Low-Income Housing Tax Credit Process.

HFAs Competitively Award Credits

HFAs competitively award tax credits to developers or owners of qualified projects that reserve all or a portion of their units for low-income tenants. HFAs award the credits in accordance with qualified allocation plans (QAP) that outline states' affordable housing priorities and ranking and selection procedures for projects.[15]

Developers Apply to HFAs for Tax Credits

To apply for tax credits, a developer must submit a detailed proposal to an HFA. To qualify for consideration, a project must meet certain requirements, such as reserving specified percentages of available units for lower-income households and restricting rents for these households to 30 percent of a calculated income limit.

Investors Provide Equity and Receive Tax Benefits

Developers typically attempt to obtain funding for their projects by attracting third-party investors willing to contribute equity financing (up-front cash) to projects. The developer sells an ownership interest in the project to one or more investors, or in some instances, to a syndicator acting as a broker between the developer and investor(s). Tax credit investors can be individuals, but the vast majority of investments have come from corporations, either investing directly or through private partnerships. Although investors buy an interest in an LIHTC partnership, this process is commonly referred to as buying tax credits because the investors receive tax credits in return for their investment (providing that the building is developed and operated according to code requirements).

Syndicators Pool Projects, Recruit Investors, and Provide Services

Syndicators, when involved, are intermediaries that often administer tax credit deals and charge a fee for overseeing the investment transaction. Syndicators pool several projects into one tax-credit equity fund and recruit investors willing to become partners in LIHTC partnerships. The investor, as a limited partner, has a large ownership percentage in the property but otherwise is not directly involved in project development. Syndicators provide legal and accounting services required to pool the tax credits, monitor projects for the investors, and sometimes fund reserves for legal and administrative costs.[16]

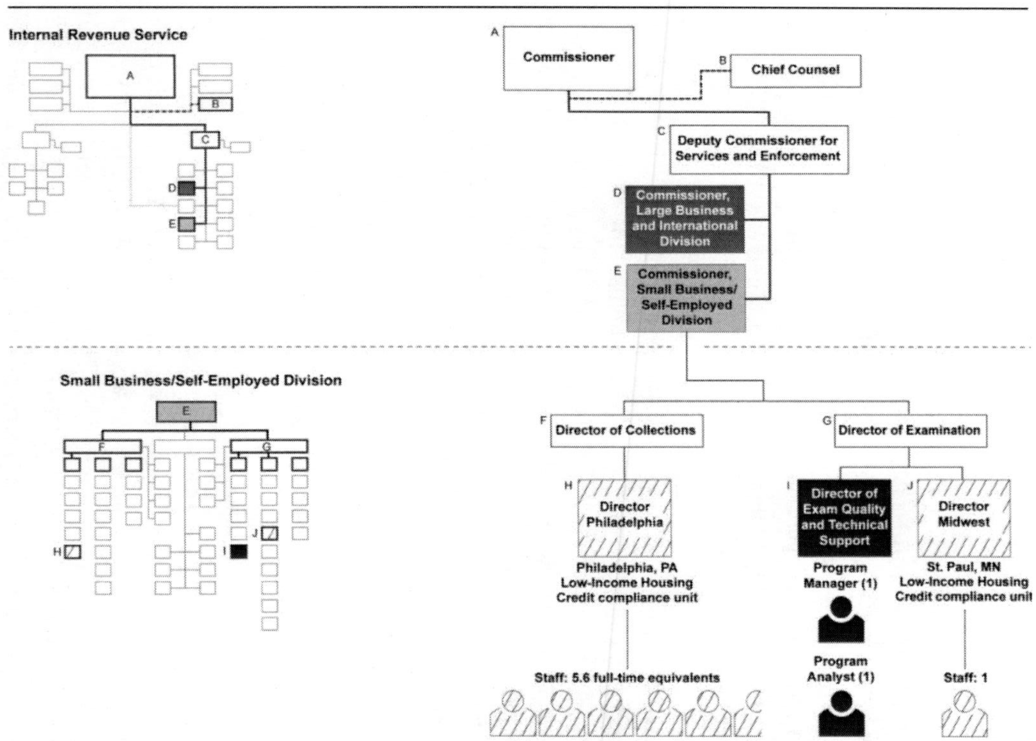

Source: Internal Revenue Service. | GAO-15-330

Figure 2. IRS Organizational Chart for the LIHTC Program, as of May 2015.

IRS Offices Involved in LIHTC Program Oversight

IRS administers the LIHTC program primarily within one division, with assistance from other offices and units (see figure 2).

- The Small Business/Self-Employed Division (SB/SE) primarily administers the LIHTC program.[17] One full-time program analyst develops internal protocols, provides technical assistance to HFAs, and provides community outreach to industry groups and taxpayers (developers/owners and investors).
- In related activities, one staff member in the Low-Income Housing Credit compliance unit (compliance unit) assists in determining if tax returns may warrant an audit. An additional 5.6 full-time equivalents, also from the compliance unit, assist in reconciling LIHTC forms from HFAs and taxpayers to identify potential inconsistencies and populate IRS's Low-Income Housing Credit database. The database has been used to record information from certain IRS forms submitted by HFAs and taxpayers.[18]
- The Office of Chief Counsel, within the Commissioner's office, provides technical assistance for the LIHTC program and determines the amount of credit available for the national pool—the amount of unused housing credit carryovers allocated to qualified states for a calendar year from a pool of unused credit. According to IRS officials, six attorneys work part-time on the LIHTC program.

IRS Responsible for Oversight of HFAs and Taxpayers, and HFAs Make Award Decisions and Monitor Projects

IRS administers the LIHTC program by developing regulations and guidance and is responsible for overseeing HFAs and taxpayer compliance. HFAs award tax credits to qualified projects, determine the credit amounts needed for financial feasibility of the projects, and monitor project compliance. The design of the LIHTC program can result in other entities—private and public—providing additional types of monitoring of LIHTC projects; examples include investors and syndicators performing due diligence in relation to a project's viability and eligibility for tax credits.

IRS Regulatory and Oversight Responsibilities for LIHTC

IRS administration of the LIHTC program involves developing and publishing regulations and guidance as well as overseeing compliance on the part of HFAs and taxpayers. The IRS Office of Chief Counsel, with assistance from Treasury's Office of Tax Policy, develops and publishes regulations and guidance based on requirements in the code. Published guidance may include revenue rulings and procedures, notices, and announcements. Other guidance for the program includes an Audit Technique Guide for Completing Form 8823—the report on noncompliance or building disposition, on which HFAs record findings after inspecting projects—and an Audit Technique Guide for Low-Income Housing Credit.[19] The guide for completing form 8823 includes specific instructions for HFAs on when desk audits, site visits, and file reviews are to be performed; how to complete the form; and guidelines for determining noncompliance in areas such as health and safety standards, rent ceilings, income limits, and tenant qualifications. The purpose of the guide is to provide standardized operational definitions of noncompliance categories. The Low-Income Housing Credit guide is a manual developed to assist IRS examiners who conduct audits of taxpayers receiving LIHTCs. The guide discusses topics ranging from examination techniques to specific issues pertinent to the LIHTC program.

IRS oversight covers allocation of LIHTCs by HFAs and taxpayer compliance (see figure 3). One full-time analyst monitors the program with assistance from the compliance unit. The compliance unit staff review information on three IRS forms that are the basis of LIHTC program reporting for HFAs and taxpayers. IRS is responsible for reviewing the forms and using them to determine whether program requirements have been met. Specifically, IRS compliance unit staff and the program analyst review the following:

- Compliance unit staff review information on credit allocation and certification (form 8609). The two-part form is completed by the HFA and the taxpayer. HFAs report the allocated amount of tax credits available over a 10-year period for each building in a project. The taxpayer reports the date on which the building was placed in service. IRS staff use a checklist to record information that might warrant additional review by the program analyst, such as discrepancies in the number of tax credits the HFA and the taxpayer reported. They also enter the information from this form in IRS's Low-Income Housing Credit database.

- The compliance unit uses a checklist to review noncompliance or building disposition (form 8823). HFAs must complete the form after conducting an on-site physical inspection of an LIHTC project if any noncompliance is found. All projects must be inspected by HFAs at least every 3 years (including at least 20 percent of low-income units). The form records any findings (and corrections of previous findings) based on the inspection of units and review of the low-income certifications. According to IRS's guide for completing form 8823, when findings are identified by HFAs and reported to IRS, the compliance unit must notify the owner of the noncompliance issues. In addition, the compliance unit determines if the identified noncompliance may warrant consideration of a taxpayer audit by IRS. If so, the compliance unit will forward an audit consideration package for the program analyst's review. The program analyst then determines the audit potential of the taxpayer. If an audit were needed, the program analyst would forward the audit package to the relevant IRS audit examination division—such as SB/SE—and monitor the status of the audit.
- The compliance unit staff review the allocations each HFA reports as having been made on the HFA annual report (form 8610) to ensure allocations do not exceed a statutorily prescribed ceiling for that year. IRS officials stated that the Office of Chief Counsel reviews all the 8610s and reports the state housing credit ceiling in published guidance for the upcoming year. HFAs also use the form to report whether they have met certain program requirements, such as confirming that their QAPs contain monitoring procedures and affirming the completion of LIHTC project monitoring. HFAs generally complete the form by the end of February of each year. The program analyst then reviews the information and follows up with HFAs as necessary.

HFAs Are Responsible for Awarding Tax Credits and Monitoring LIHTC Projects

IRS relies on HFAs to administer and oversee the LIHTC program in their states.[20] In addition to awarding tax credits to qualified projects, HFAs are responsible for:

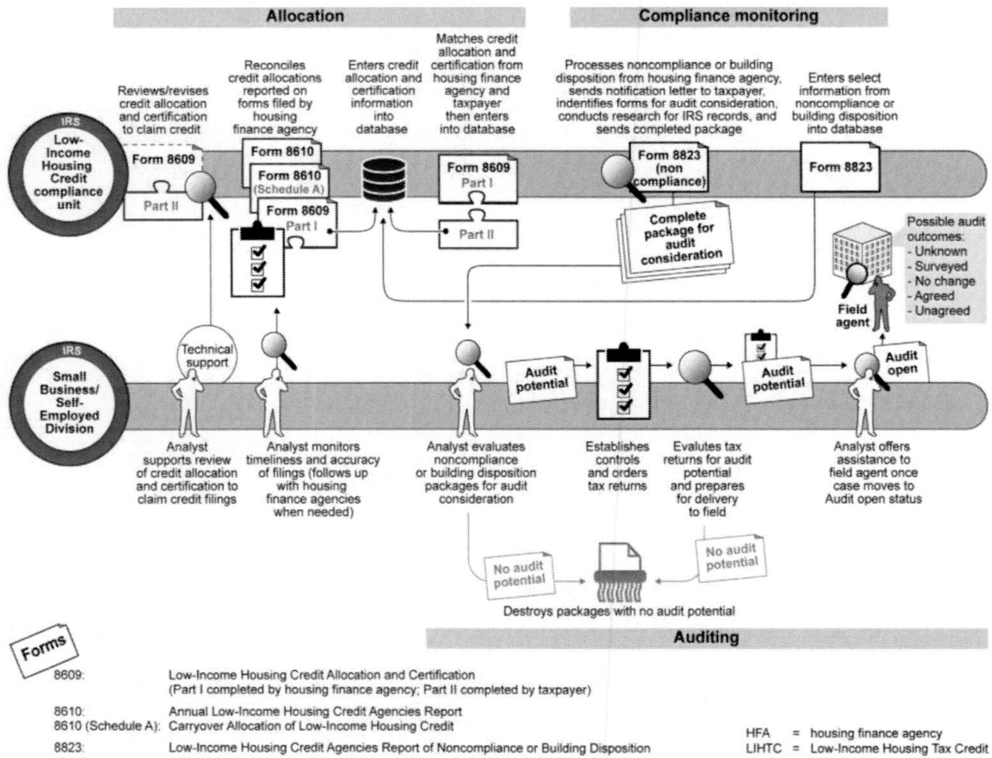

Source: GAO. | GAO-15-330

Figure 3. IRS Oversight Responsibilities for HFA and Taxpayer LIHTC Allocations and Compliance Monitoring by HFAs.

- determining the amount of credit needed for the financial feasibility of each project and its viability as a qualified low-income housing project through the 10-year credit period. HFAs make determinations (1) when the application is received, (2) when the allocation of the credit is completed, and (3) when the building is placed in service and the taxpayer submits a final cost certification.
- monitoring LIHTC properties for compliance with program requirements (for example, health and safety standards, rent ceilings, income limits, and tenant qualifications). Findings from HFA monitoring are provided to IRS on noncompliance or building disposition (form 8823). Taxpayer noncompliance with LIHTC requirements may result in IRS denying claims for the credit in the current year or recapturing—taking back—credits claimed in prior years.

Once IRS monitoring of LIHTC projects ends after year 15, HFAs have sole authority to monitor compliance for at least another 15 years, and the taxpayer must ensure that the project continues to meet program requirements, as defined in the project's extended use agreement with the HFA. If a project were found to be noncompliant, the HFA could take action, such as litigation under state law.

LIHTC Projects Also May Be Monitored by Other Entities

The design of the LIHTC program (for instance, the roles of investors and syndicators) can result in other entities—private and public—providing additional types of monitoring of LIHTC projects. Investors and syndicators not only provide financing for LIHTC projects, but also provide project oversight to help ensure that they receive the expected tax credits over the designated period. For instance, an LIHTC investor needs to make sure the property is suitable for occupancy and rented to qualified low-income families at restricted rents during the initial 15-year period. To mitigate risk before investing, the investor and syndicators will underwrite and screen properties for quality and sustainability. For example, the investor may ensure the development team has adequate resources to build and operate the property and that mechanisms are in place to avoid foreclosure. Additionally, because of the amount of capital that can be involved in projects, investors may require additional testing and auditing beyond what is required by the program.

Investors and syndicators also may maintain a list of properties to more closely monitor based on identified performance measures. However, findings from investors and syndicators typically are not shared with the public or federal agencies, according to Treasury officials.

LIHTC projects also can receive funds from other federal programs and be subject to monitoring requirements of those programs—for example, HUD's HOME and project-based Section 8 rental assistance programs.[21] According to a 2012 industry survey of HFAs with LIHTC projects that received other federal funds, an average of about 20 percent of the units received HOME funds and an average of about 18 percent received project-based Section 8 rental assistance.[22] The monitoring conducted for the other programs provides additional information that could be useful for IRS in monitoring LIHTC projects. However, IRS officials stated they do not review findings on HFAs that other programs identified but rather focus on ensuring completion and submission of IRS tax forms. Examples of monitoring requirements from these programs include the following:

- For HOME, HUD requires that participating jurisdictions conduct on-site physical inspections of projects every 1, 2, or 3 years, depending on the size of the project. These site visits also require reviews of program and project files. HUD approves the use of grant funds by reviewing a state or locality's consolidated plan, which identifies needs, sets priorities, determines resources, and sets goals.
- For project-based Section 8 rental assistance, performance-based contract administrators (entities such as HFAs and public housing authorities) assist HUD in overseeing individual Section 8 properties and ensure that properties are in compliance with HUD policies. The contract administrators must perform annual management and occupancy reviews for all their assigned properties and conduct monthly reviews of all payment vouchers submitted by property owners. For example, the contract administrators conduct on-site reviews of property owners' tenant information files and ensure property owners provide complete and accurate tenant data to HUD. HUD's oversight of the contract administrators can include reviews of status reports of performance-based administrators and annual compliance reviews, which determine the compensation of the contract administrator.[23]

In addition to specific program requirements, HUD program participants must comply with several federal civil rights requirements, including the Fair Housing Act and Americans with Disabilities Act.[24] Such requirements prohibit discrimination in the administration of housing subsidies and require buildings to be designed and constructed in an accessible manner, located in appropriate sites and neighborhoods, and marketed equally to all potential tenants. For certain requirements, officials told us that HUD routinely monitors program participants. For others, HUD uses an administrative complaint procedure to identify candidates for reviews. HUD's monitoring consists of a combination of file reviews and site visits.

HFAs also have used funding from the Tax Credit Assistance Program (TCAP), administered by HUD, and the Grants to States for Low-Income Housing Projects in Lieu of Low-Income Housing Credits (Section 1602) program, administered by Treasury. The LIHTC program was severely disrupted in 2008–2009 (in the midst of the financial crisis), when the demand for the credits and the price investors were willing to pay for them declined. TCAP and Section 1602 provided gap financing to fill the equity gap that resulted from lower LIHTC prices, allowing stalled "shovel-ready" projects to proceed.[25] The two programs no longer actively fund new projects, but as of May 2015, compliance monitoring of funded projects remained ongoing.

The TCAP and 1602 programs require more compliance monitoring than traditional LIHTC projects; for example, of asset-management functions the HFAs perform.[26] HUD and Treasury also have used a risk-based approach to monitor TCAP and 1602 projects. For example, HUD determined that TCAP projects that had less than $10,000 in LIHTC investment and no other federal funding sources might be at higher risk of noncompliance. HUD officials explained these TCAP projects were considered higher-risk due to the potential of less oversight from other private and public entities. Treasury reviewed HFAs for compliance in the first year of the Section 1602 program. Then Treasury used a risk-based approach to identify HFAs for subsequent reviews (they would merit additional monitoring if noncompliance issues were identified in the first review). Thereafter, on an annual basis during the compliance period, HFAs have to certify to Treasury that they performed all required compliance monitoring activities and report to Treasury the results of these activities for each project.

Finally, unlike LIHTC, some of these grant programs—HOME, project-based Section 8 rental assistance, and TCAP—are considered federal financial assistance by the Single Audit Act, and thus are subject to an annual single audit by a third party.[27] Annual external audits must include a review of financial statements and internal controls and adherence to program compliance requirements.

IRS Oversight to Identify and Address Compliance Issues has been Minimal

IRS performed minimal oversight of HFAs, particularly in relation to reviewing QAPs and assessing HFA compliance. IRS conducted some audits of taxpayers claiming the tax credits, but does not have detailed information on the results of these audits. Moreover, IRS has not set goals or assessed performance for the program. Finally, data in IRS's Low-Income Housing Credit database were not complete and reliable for assessing compliance.

IRS Oversight of HFAs has been Minimal

IRS oversight of HFAs has been minimal, particularly in terms of reviewing QAPs and conducting on-site or desk audits of HFAs. Federal internal control standards state that internal control helps program managers achieve desired results.[28] Monitoring, one of the internal control standards, should occur in the course of normal operations, be performed continually, and be ingrained in the agency's operations.

IRS officials stated they did not regularly review QAPs as part of their compliance monitoring of the HFA annual report (form 8610).[29] IRS's review of HFAs included a review of responses on the annual report related to compliance monitoring procedures in the QAP and frequency of monitoring conducted by the HFA. However, in addition to these requirements, the code includes requirements for selecting projects and ensuring a QAP is approved by the state governing agency.[30] Yet, IRS has not conducted regular reviews of QAPs to determine how HFAs interpreted the code to select projects, if the QAPs included the required compliance monitoring, or if the QAPs had been approved. As a result of minimal monitoring, IRS does not know the extent of compliance monitoring by HFAs, which limits its ability to determine if the HFAs appropriately awarded credits to projects.[31]

Moreover, IRS and Treasury were unclear about how to handle instances in which a QAP did not meet requirements in the code. Some Treasury and IRS officials stated that Treasury would have to invalidate all credits allocated to an HFA if the QAP did not meet requirements, which could affect awarded projects across multiple years. In contrast, IRS has reported in audit-related documents that an HFA's authority to allocate tax credits should be revoked only when IRS determined that the HFA's noncompliance was widespread and willful. The documents suggest that such revocation most likely would be applied prospectively to limit the tax consequences for taxpayers.

IRS has performed few on-site or desk audits of the 56 HFAs—it audited a total of 7 HFAs—from the program's inception in 1986 through May 2015.[32] According to an IRS summary report of all HFA audits conducted from 2003 to 2014, the agency generally selected which HFAs to audit based on press accounts and HFA self-reporting about lack of adherence with compliance requirements.[33] IRS officials also stated that HFAs increasingly have missed the February 28 deadline to submit the annual report (form 8610) and often submit incomplete or inaccurate forms. The summary report recognized that conducting ongoing audits is a necessary component of LIHTC program administration. The report also notes continued audit presence would reinforce the importance of HFA compliance with requirements in the code and provide an opportunity for IRS to address deliberate noncompliance by HFAs.

The scope and methods of the reviews varied based on the types of noncompliance the IRS program analyst identified. For instance, on one audit the program analyst selected a sample of files on which to conduct an in-depth review of HFA compliance activities. In another, the program analyst enlisted the assistance of a field agent to review the HFA's internal controls for record keeping and credit allocation, among other areas. The other audits were desk audits. Examples of the audit findings include the following:

- Written HFA policies conflicted with the requirements in the code or Treasury regulations.
- The QAP did not address all compliance requirements in the regulations or was outdated.
- Annual report to IRS had errors, such as incorrect credit allocations and overstated numbers of inspections and reviews.
- The HFA failed to submit form 8823 as required to report LIHTC noncompliance.
- Physical inspections and tenant file reviews were not completed as required and notifications to owners were not conducted as required.

All but one audit was closed at the time of our review.

IRS cited multiple reasons for not conducting regular reviews of QAPs and audits of HFAs. First, IRS officials stated that they did not regard a regular review of QAPs as a part of their compliance responsibilities. Second, IRS officials stated that because of other priorities the agency does not have a sufficient number of LIHTC staff or other assigned resources to conduct more audits of HFAs. IRS has statutory authority to collect up to a $100 annual penalty from each HFA failing to file a timely, accurate annual report. However, IRS officials said the agency concluded that penalty collection would not be cost-effective because more resources would be needed to collect the penalty than would be gained through collection and that increasing the penalty amount would require statutory change. Third, IRS officials stated that they had considered involving IRS field office staff to conduct more HFA audits over the years, but due to competing demands at IRS, this did not occur. The lack of QAP reviews and audits of HFAs means that IRS is unable to determine the extent to which HFAs meet requirements for awarding tax credits and monitoring project compliance.

IRS has Conducted Some Audits of Taxpayers Claiming LIHTCs but does not have Detailed Information on Results of these Audits

IRS has conducted some audits of taxpayers claiming LIHTCs, but does not have detailed information on these audits. In a 1997 report, we found that IRS did not have an estimate of taxpayer compliance for the LIHTC program and recommended that IRS explore alternative ways to evaluate compliance with the requirements of the code by taxpayers.[34] In 2000, IRS had completed a review of a sample of 402 audits of LIHTC taxpayers performed from 1995 through 1999 (an average of about 100 audits annually to determine a compliance level by taxpayers claiming the credit and types of noncompliance).[35] According to IRS, the review did not find evidence of widespread noncompliance with the code. Officials also stated the agency had not updated this review since 2000—15 years ago—because IRS had been proceeding with the understanding that nothing had changed with the compliance level.

According to IRS, the agency completed 555 additional audits (an average of about 40 audits annually) of taxpayers claiming LIHTCs from 2001 through 2013. About 29 percent of these audits resulted in no change to the amount of credit claimed by the taxpayer or recapture of the credit. For the remaining audits, the taxpayer agreed to make changes to the credit claimed (about 24 percent); IRS no longer pursued the case (about 23 percent)—for example, because the statute of limitation was within 1 year of expiring; IRS continued to audit the taxpayer (about 10 percent); or IRS closed the case because the taxpayer disagreed with the audit results and requested adjudication (about 10 percent).[36] According to IRS officials, competing audit priorities have limited the number of LIHTC taxpayer audits conducted.

Detailed information on the results of the audits of taxpayers claiming LIHTCs have not been shared with LIHTC staff. More specifically, IRS examiners have not provided information on types and trends in noncompliance or the amount of credit changed or recaptured. In June 2002, we concluded that tracking audit findings and identifying commonly occurring issues could be valuable in helping management evaluate agency oversight, monitor activities, and identify problem areas.[37] Moreover, we have consistently stressed the importance of IRS conducting tax compliance research to understand the extent and causes of taxpayer noncompliance and use the results to review audit examination programs.[38] LIHTC staff stated they have not maintained a database on outcomes of audits (such as types of and trends in noncompliance), the recapture of tax credits or adjustments of credit for compliance monitoring purposes, or coordinated within IRS to monitor recapture of the program credit. As a result, information on commonly occurring issues and reasons for taxpayer noncompliance related to the LIHTC program is not available to inform the program analyst responsible for overseeing the program.

IRS has not set Goals for LIHTC and does not Assess Performance

Although IRS is the only federal agency responsible for overseeing LIHTC program compliance, it does not set goals or assess performance for the program. Federal internal control standards state activities need to be established to monitor performance measures and indicators, which includes comparing data so that analyses can be conducted, as appropriate.[39] We previously reported that data availability was a challenge in assessing tax expenditure performance.[40] IRS collects limited data that it needs to administer and enforce the code. It does not use the information it collects to assess the housing production program, such as the number and location of LIHTC projects. (We discuss IRS's Low-Income Housing Credit database in more detail later in this report.)

HUD's role in the LIHTC program is generally limited to the collection of information on tenant characteristics (mandated by the Housing and Economic Recovery Act of 2008). However, it has voluntarily collected project-level information on the program since 1996 because of the importance of LIHTC as a source of funding for affordable housing. HUD also has sponsored studies of the LIHTC program that use these data. HUD's LIHTC databases, the largest federal source of information on the LIHTC program, aggregate project-level data voluntarily submitted by HFAs and the tenant characteristic information HUD must collect. In our December 2012 report on the LIHTC program, we found that HUD's LIHTC databases were incomplete and missing data on many projects.[41] We recommended HUD evaluate and implement additional steps to improve the database, which could improve the federal government's ability to evaluate basic LIHTC program outcomes. HUD agreed and has since implemented our recommendation by taking steps to identify potential gaps in its database. For example, in December 2014, HUD published a report analyzing data it must collect on tenants residing in LIHTC properties.[42] As part of this report, HUD compared property information in its tenant database to the information in its property database to help assess the completeness of both databases.

Furthermore, HUD has been limited in its ability to report complete information on how the LIHTC program contributed toward meeting agency priority goals and broader, federal housing goals. The Office of Management and Budget's 2014 guidance on content for strategic plans, annual performance plans, and annual performance reports directs agencies to include tax expenditures in their identification of organizations and programs that contribute to agency priority goals (areas of special focus as determined by the agency administration).[43] HUD has strategic goals to meet the need for quality affordable rental homes and build strong resilient and inclusive communities. HUD also has a priority goal to preserve and expand affordable rental housing. HUD's fiscal year 2013 annual performance report and 2015 annual performance plan included a performance measure that accounted for LIHTC projects with HUD- insured mortgages in its agency priority goal. Overall, HUD's goals call for continuing to assist about 5.5 million households living in subsidized housing and serving approximately 62,000 additional households through affordable rental housing programs.[44] However, officials said data used to support these goals do not include all LIHTC units, but only those units that have HUD mortgage insurance. HUD has a separate process for collecting LIHTC information for HUD-insured properties and does not rely on any of the existing databases on LIHTC.

In our May 2011 glossary on performance measurement and evaluation, we stated that performance measurement can serve as an early warning system to program management because of its ongoing nature and as a vehicle for improving performance and accountability to the public.[45] Information about the extent to which an intended purpose has been met also can contribute towards broader evaluations of how well a program has been working and actions that could be taken to improve results. Basic information on results, such as the number and location of LIHTC projects, is limited. Without goals and performance measures, decision makers do not have sufficient information to assess the results or the effectiveness of the program as a tool to maintain affordable housing.

IRS Data Were Not Reliable to Assess Compliance and Taxpayer Protections Prevent HUD from Using IRS Data

IRS had not comprehensively captured information reported for the program in its Low-Income Housing Credit database and the existing data were not complete and reliable. IRS guidance requires the collection of data on the LIHTC program in an IRS database. The IRS database records information submitted by HFAs and taxpayers on three forms—credit allocation and certification (form 8609), HFA report of noncompliance or building disposition (form 8823), and HFA annual reports (form 8610)—and IRS mainly uses the data to reconcile program information submitted and identify taxpayers for audit.[46]

Data on Credit Allocation and Certification not Reliable

Based on our analysis of the information in the database, the data on credit allocation and certification information were not sufficiently reliable to determine if basic requirements for the LIHTC program were being achieved.[47] Federal internal control standards state that effective information technology management is critical to achieving useful, reliable, and continuous recording and communication of information.[48] However, our electronic testing of IRS data found instances in which allocation dates and placed-in-service dates were incorrectly entered in the database, which highlighted problems with how the data elements were entered into the database from paper forms. Automatic edit checks to ensure that the date fields entered are reasonable were not fully implemented, although IRS's database user guide describes the use of such checks. Officials stated they did not become aware that the edit checks were not working until our assessment of the data. The programming of the edit checks contained errors, which prevented them from working correctly. IRS officials agreed that these problems should be corrected and data quality reviews conducted on an ongoing basis. Because IRS has not regularly assessed the credit allocation and certification information (form 8609) for errors and conducted management review of the data, we could not determine how often LIHTC projects were placed in service within required time frames. Without improvements to the data quality of credit allocation and certification information, it is difficult to determine if credit allocation and placed-in-service requirements have been met by HFAs and taxpayers, respectively.

Moreover, we found IRS guidance requires information from the HFA report of noncompliance or building disposition (form 8823) and the HFA annual reports (form 8610) to be captured in the Low-Income Housing Credit database. However, based on our review of the database, the information was partially captured for the noncompliance form and not captured for the HFA annual reports.

- More specifically, we could not determine the types or frequency of project noncompliance from data available on the HFA reports on noncompliance or building disposition (form 8823). According to IRS, the agency has received approximately 168,000 noncompliance or building disposition forms since 2009 but the database included about 3,100 records (about 2 percent of records received). Officials told us the decision was made in 2008–2009 to input information only from forms that indicated a change in building disposition, such as the foreclosure of a project. IRS focused on forms indicating a change because of the serious nature of these occurrences for the program, the impacts on taxpayers' ability to receive credit, and greater prevalence of these occurrences as a result of the economic downturn. Additionally, when IRS upgraded its database in 2008 a large backlog of un-entered information existed (the database was offline from 2005 to 2008); however, officials realized their operations were not affected by the lack of information. Officials further explained it was not cost-effective to input information received from all forms 8823 into the

database because the need for trend analysis on all types of noncompliance was not useful for purposes of ensuring compliance with the tax code. However, officials stated they have not performed any cost estimates to determine the cost of inputting such information.
- The database does not contain information from HFA annual reports (form 8610). IRS officials stated there were plans to include this information in the database from 2009 to the present, but due to competing priorities for limited resources, it has not yet been added.

Restrictions on Information Sharing

Statutory restrictions in the Internal Revenue Code prevent the disclosure of taxpayer information to other federal agencies, such as HUD, that may make more use of the data.[49] For LIHTC, taxpayer protections restricting disclosure of taxpayer information generally prohibit IRS from sharing data it collects on the LIHTC program with HUD. HUD officials said they experienced difficulties obtaining data from IRS to help ensure the completeness of their data because of issues related to protections for taxpayer information.[50] The code does not specifically give IRS the authority to provide information to HUD so that HUD can assess the completeness of the data it receives from HFAs on tenant characteristics or other data elements in HUD's LIHTC database for the program.

Nevertheless, Congress has granted some statutory exceptions to the provisions relating to confidentiality while balancing the expectation of taxpayer privacy with the policy goals of efficient use of federal resources, public health and welfare, and law enforcement.[51] IRS staff suggested internally that Congress create such an exception for the LIHTC program, authorizing IRS to provide HUD with protected information on LIHTC buildings and enabling HUD to assess the completeness of the LIHTC tenant information it collects. In that case, HUD could then review its databases, compare the information against the IRS data, determine what information it was missing on tenant characteristics, and follow up with the HFA as necessary. According to officials, neither IRS management nor Treasury (which must present all administration proposed tax legislation) has yet received this internal proposal.

Table 1. Overview of Administrative Structures, Monitoring, and Performance Measurement of Three Tax Credit Programs

	Low-Income Housing Tax Credit	Historic Rehabilitation Tax Credit	New Markets Tax Credit
Administrative structure			
Federal entity (other than IRS) with formal administrative role	N/A[a]	Technical Preservation Services (TPS) in the National Park Service	Community Development Financial Institutions Fund in theDepartment of the Treasury
State entity with formal administrative role	Housing finance agency (HFA)	State Historic Preservation Officer	N/A[a]
Private-sector entity with an oversight role	Investors/Syndicators	Investors/Syndicators	Community Development Entity (entity that awards the tax credits in return for equity investments)
Monitoring			
IRS	IRS audits of selected taxpayers claiming credit.	IRS audits of selected taxpayers claiming credit.	IRS audits of selected taxpayers claiming credit.
Federal partner entity	N/A[a]	TPS conducts oversight of State Historic Preservation Officers, through approximately 25 work trips per year to states, which may involve on-site inspections of multiple projects.	Community Development Financial Institutions Fund performs programmatic- and risk-based compliance site visits of Community Development Entities.
State partner entity	HFAs monitor LIHTC properties for compliance with program requirements through desk audits, site visits, and file reviews.[b]	State Historic Preservation Officers monitor projects during a 5-year compliance period. Frequency of monitoring is determined on an as-needed basis.	N/A[a]
Private-sector partner entity	Investors/syndicators may perform oversight of property management and operations to ensure	Investors/syndicators may perform oversight of property management	Community Development Entities monitoring of investments may include review of financial reports,

	Low-Income Housing Tax Credit	Historic Rehabilitation Tax Credit	New Markets Tax Credit
	compliance and viability of LIHTC property.	and operations to ensure compliance and viability of property.	semiannual site visits, annual interviews, and brief surveys.
Performance measurement			
IRS	N/A[a]	N/A[a]	N/A[a]
Federal partner entity	N/A[a,c]	TPS publishes annual reports and annual statistical reports; collaborates with Rutgers University on annual economic impact report.	Community Development Financial Institutions Fund produces annual research reports and periodic research briefs; contracted with Urban Institute to conduct a formal evaluation of the program.
State partner entity	N/A[a]	N/A[a,d]	N/A[a]
Private-sector partner entity	Unknown[e]	Unknown[e]	Unknown[e]

Source: GAO analysis of LIHTC, Historic Rehabilitation Tax Credit, and New Markets Tax Credit information. | GAO-15-330

[a] Not applicable means that no requirement is in place.

[b] At least once every 3 years, HFAs must perform on-site physical inspections for all buildings in a project and, for at least 20 percent of low-income units, inspect the units and review the income certifications of tenants.

[c] HUD collects data on LIHTC projects from HFAs, on a voluntary basis. In addition, HUD collects information on tenant characteristics as required by the Housing and Economic Recovery Act of 2008. HUD also has an agency priority goal for preserving and expanding affordable housing and tracks LIHTC units occupied for this goal; however, the information included on LIHTC units is not complete.

[d] Officials stated that State Historic Preservation Officers and their partners, although not required to do so, may have published reports on the economic impact and other public benefits of the Historic Rehabilitation Tax Credit in their states.

[e] We did not review whether private-sector entities collect performance measures. As noted previously, LIHTC investors and syndicators monitor projects; however, according to Treasury officials, limited data are available to the public on this activity.

LIHTC Administration Differs from Some Other Tax Credit Programs

LIHTC administration differs from some other tax credit programs that are jointly administered by IRS with another federal agency. The other federal agencies conduct monitoring, report on performance, collect data, and have missions consistent with the purposes of the programs. HUD's experience in affordable housing and working with HFAs may benefit the LIHTC program. More specifically, HUD's rental housing programs rely on state and local housing agencies (including HFAs) to implement programs. A greater involvement of HUD in the LIHTC program may help alleviate the oversight challenges cited in this report. But joint federal administration may require additional resources for HUD.

IRS Jointly Administers Some Tax Credit Programs with Other Federal Agencies

In some cases, IRS jointly administers tax credit programs with other federal agencies that provide key oversight and administrative support, such as monitoring, performance measurement, and data collection. Specifically, we identified two programs—the Historic Rehabilitation Tax Credit and the New Markets Tax Credit—in which federal administration of the programs is shared between IRS and another agency (see table 1 for overview).[52]

Historic Rehabilitation Tax Credit Program

The Historic Rehabilitation Tax Credit program promotes the rehabilitation of historic properties. For this credit, developers planning to rehabilitate "certified historic structures"—buildings listed in the National Register of Historic Places or located in a registered historic district and certified by the National Park Service (NPS) as contributing to the historic significance of that district—can apply for certification to NPS through their local State Historic Preservation Officer for tax credits in the amount of 20 percent of the certified rehabilitation costs.

Source: GAO. | GAO-15-330

We discuss the Historic Rehabilitation Tax Credit and the New Markets Tax Credit programs in greater detail below, focusing on differences with how IRS oversees LIHTC—such as describing how the other federal entities monitor and assess program performance.

Historic Rehabilitation Tax Credit

The National Park Service's Technical Preservation Services (TPS) administers the Historic Rehabilitation Tax Credit program, which cost an estimated $580 million in forgone revenue in fiscal year 2014. TPS promulgates the Secretary ofthe Interior's Standards for Rehabilitation (standards), to which renovation projects must conform to be eligible for rehabilitation tax credits. TPS, in consultation with State Historic Preservation Officers (SHPO), also reviews and approves proposed rehabilitation project designs, and (again in consultation with SHPOs) certifies completed rehabilitation projects as conforming to the standards and therefore eligible to claim the rehabilitation tax credit.

NEW MARKETS TAX CREDIT PROGRAM

Congress established the New Markets Tax Credit to encourage investments in low- income communities that traditionally lack access to capital. The program provides investors (individuals, financial institutions, and other corporations) with a tax credit for investing in these communities. The investors can claim a credit equal to 39 percent of eligible investment spread over 7 years.

Source: GAO. | GAO-15-330

TPS officials explained that to administer the Historic Rehabilitation Tax Credit program, the agency currently relies on 17 full-time equivalent positions to staff the program and has a budget of approximately $3.2 million for fiscal year 2015. Additionally, TPS officials stated they planned to add 4–5 full-time equivalent positions to the program, for a total of 21 or 22. TPS officials explained that they work with IRS to coordinate elements of program administration, which include the issuance of regulations, the development of program information (such as on revenue procedures) for TPS's website, and training for SHPOs. TPS also shares program data with IRS, including biannual reports of all program activity drawn from the project database for the

Historic Rehabilitation Tax Credit, and information about issues and concerns surrounding an individual project's eligibility for the credit.[53]

New Markets Tax Credit

The CDFI Fund, housed in Treasury, plays the lead role in administering the New Markets Tax Credit program, which had about $1 billion in forgone revenue in fiscal year 2014. The Fund certifies qualified organizations as Community Development Entities (CDE)—which are entitled to offer these tax credits to investors to attract private-equity investments to low-income community development projects. The Fund also reviews CDE applications for allocations of specific amounts of the New Markets Tax Credit and—for those CDEs receiving such allocations—prepares allocation agreements that include the amount of tax credit allocation, approved uses of the allocation, approved service area, and reporting requirements.

According to CDFI Fund officials, 15 full-time equivalent positions—14 staff and one manager—work full time on New Markets Tax Credit and another Treasury program, with the majority of staff time devoted to New Markets Tax Credits. These employees are assisted at various times by other CDFI Fund staff—for example, legal staff who help to execute allocation agreements with CDEs and information technology staff who maintain database systems.

In both programs, we identified oversight and administrative functions (monitoring, performance measurement, and data collection) that federal entities other than IRS perform.[54]

Monitoring

TPS and the CDFI Fund have primary roles in monitoring programmatic aspects of the Historic Rehabilitation Tax Credit and New Markets Tax Credit, while IRS administers and enforces compliance with tax-related requirements. Conversely, in the LIHTC program, the monitoring role is split between IRS and HFAs. While IRS has other monitoring responsibilities for the LIHTC program (beyond ensuring taxpayer compliance) that include overseeing HFAs, as discussed previously, such monitoring was lacking or minimal.

Historic Rehabilitation Tax Credit

TPS officials told us that TPS staff members take approximately 25 work trips annually to states for purposes such as site visits and training for SHPOs. Site visits typically involve inspections of multiple projects, including projects identified as good and as problematic, as well as projects that are proposed, under way, and completed. TPS officials stated that when they identify deficiencies in a SHPO's administration of a Historic Rehabilitation Tax Credit project, they generally work cooperatively with SHPOs to identify and take corrective actions.

New Markets Tax Credit

CDFI Fund staff told us they conduct two types of site visits to CDEs that are performed by different program offices.

- The New Markets Tax Credit program office conducts site visits to gather information about current industry practices, tax credit transaction costs, best practices in accomplishing outcomes the CDFI Fund seeks to encourage (such as investing in nonmetropolitan counties and financing projects that create significant community outcomes), and emerging trends and practices the CDFI Fund may want to discourage. The information obtained during these site visits enables the New Markets Tax Credit staff to administer the program by informing the contents of the tax credit allocation application or allocation agreement, or the review and selection process.
- The Certification, Compliance Monitoring and Evaluation unit conducts risk-based site visits. The purpose of these visits includes determining if a New Markets Tax Credit project was in compliance with the terms and conditions of its allocation agreement, assessing circumstances leading to an instance of noncompliance, and identifying any weaknesses or concerns that may adversely affect the use of the tax credit allocation. If noncompliance were in question, the focus of the site visit would be to determine what, if any, corrective actions were taken by the CDE and progress made in resolving the noncompliance, implementing the corrective action, or both.

Performance Measures and Data Collection

TPS and the CDFI Fund collect and report performance measures and collect data for the Historic Rehabilitation Tax Credit and New Markets Tax Credit programs, respectively. In contrast, IRS does not report on performance measures on the LIHTC program; rather, it collects data from tax forms to oversee HFA program compliance and taxpayer compliance. As discussed previously, statutory limitations prevent the sharing of data from tax forms with other federal agencies.

Historic Rehabilitation Tax Credit

TPS publishes an annual report and a statistical analysis of the Historic Rehabilitation Tax Credit program.[55] Both reports include performance measures such as the number of jobs created in association with completed projects and the number of housing units created with Historic Rehabilitation Tax Credits, including the number of low- and moderate-income units. The statistical analysis contains additional detail about the performance measures, historical data, and state-by-state breakdowns related to qualified rehabilitation expenditures. In addition, TPS collaborates with Rutgers University to produce the Annual Report on the Economic Impact of the Federal Historic Tax Credit.[56] According to TPS officials, to produce these reports, TPS uses data obtained from the project applications, voluntary user profiles, and customer satisfaction questionnaires submitted upon project completion.[57] TPS— unlike HUD in relation to the LIHTC program—has not encountered data-sharing limitations with IRS stemming from protections on taxpayer information because it collects these data using its own forms and documentation.

New Markets Tax Credit

The CDFI Fund uses its Community Investment Impact System to collect data from CDEs on projects, including performance measures such as the number of jobs by type; numbers of rental and for-sale housing units; and the capacity of educational, child care, and health care facilities developed using New Markets Tax Credit financing. These data are not collected on IRS forms. The data are used to produce annual research reports and periodic research briefs. In addition, the CDFI Fund contracted with the Urban Institute to conduct a formal evaluation of the New Markets Tax Credit program, focusing on program design, execution, outputs, and outcomes.[58]

HUD's Experience in Affordable Housing and Working with HFAs May Benefit the LIHTC Program

While multiple federal agencies administer housing-related programs, HUD is the lead federal agency for providing affordable rental housing.[59] HUD's fiscal year 2013 annual performance report and 2015 annual performance plan reported that it funded about 5.5 million occupied affordable rental units through its rental assistance programs.[60] Much like LIHTC, HUD's rental housing programs rely on state and local housing agencies (including HFAs) to implement programs. HUD is responsible for overseeing these agencies, including reviewing state and local consolidated plans for the HOME and Community Development Block Grant (CDBG) programs—large grant programs that HUD oversees and that also are used to fund LIHTC projects.[61] HUD has experience in directly overseeing HFAs in their roles as contract administrators for project-based Section 8 rental assistance. HUD also has entered into risk-sharing agreements with HFAs to provide more insurance on multifamily loans.[62] Although we and HUD's Office of Inspector General have identified weaknesses in evaluation and oversight of programs, HUD has taken steps to resolve some of these issues. Furthermore, HUD has processes, procedures, and staff in place for program evaluation and oversight of state and local agencies that could be built upon and strengthened.

HUD already has a limited data collection role in the LIHTC program. As described earlier, HUD voluntarily maintains data on LIHTC properties and must collect data on tenant characteristics such as race and income. Unlike IRS, HUD also has sponsored studies of the LIHTC program based on the data it collects. Furthermore, HUD has strategic goals to meet the need for quality, affordable rental homes and build strong resilient and inclusive communities, and an agency priority goal to preserve and expand affordable rental housing. However, data used to support these goals do not include all LIHTC projects. With the exception of these activities, HUD has no statutory authority to oversee HFAs' LIHTC program responsibilities or set LIHTC program policies and procedures, and as a result, such authority would require new enabling legislation.

HUD's experience in administering affordable housing programs may help address some of the oversight challenges for LIHTC cited in this report. Although joint administration of the program will involve dividing responsibilities for one program across two agencies, we have reported that mission fragmentation and program overlap sometimes may be necessary when the resources and expertise of more than one agency are required to address a complex public need—as in the case of the Historic Rehabilitation Tax Credit and New Markets Tax Credit programs.[63] HUD officials indicated that a larger role in the LIHTC program would be one way to aid their data collection efforts, better determine whether national affordable housing and fair housing goals had been incorporated, and better coordinate monitoring of civil rights compliance among federal housing programs.

IRS also has been challenged to focus on its core mission of helping taxpayers understand and meet their responsibilities and enforcing tax laws. IRS's enforcement of tax laws has been on our high-risk list since 1990.[64] In February 2015, we determined that significant capacity challenges—such as reduced staffing and examination coverage in an environment of constrained budgets—and incomplete monitoring of enforcement program performance have prevented the removal of the agency from the high-risk list.[65] Moreover, since 2010, the IRS budget has been reduced about 10 percent and IRS enforcement performance and staffing levels have declined. And as we discussed previously in this report, LIHTC receives a small portion of those resources. IRS and Treasury officials further noted that oversight of individual state HFAs that award tax credits and monitor projects is a challenge given IRS's mission of helping taxpayers meet their responsibilities and enforcing tax laws.

Joint Administration May Require Additional HUD Resources

Assigning LIHTC programmatic oversight responsibilities to another agency could involve additional staff and other resources. Specifically, such oversight responsibilities likely will involve new hiring as well as training of new and existing staff. According to HUD officials, HUD currently works with HFAs in various capacities, including administering HOME and other housing programs. However, an expanded oversight role in LIHTC would require additional resources. For example, resources would be needed to expand or build data systems to help HUD monitor HFAs and program performance. As noted earlier, HUD was statutorily required in 2008 to collect data on characteristics, such as race and income, of tenants living in LIHTC projects. HUD officials noted that collecting such data was challenging because HUD did not receive additional resources.[66]

In our review of LIHTC and the other two tax credit programs, we found that each used different mechanisms to fund their administrative responsibilities. For instance, the Historic Rehabilitation Tax Credit uses fees to fund its administrative activities, such as issuance of regulations, the development of program information, and monitoring.[67] In contrast, the New Markets Tax Credit does not rely on user fees but receives annual appropriations to fund its activities, such as application reviews, monitoring, and performance measurement.

For LIHTC, the HFAs partially fund their administration and oversight responsibilities—which include ongoing compliance inspections and other reviews—by assessing fees on owners of LIHTC projects. While practices can differ among the states, according to an annual survey by NCSHA, HFAs can assess a variety of fees to help offset their administrative costs, including application fees, reservation fees, carryover allocation fees, compliance monitoring fees, and penalties and fees related to late or amended submissions.[68] The amounts of these fees vary from state to state; for example, LIHTC application fees range from $0 in Alaska to $6,500 in Georgia.[69]

The level of resources that would be needed to perform an adequate level of oversight of HFAs is not known. According to HUD officials, estimating the level of resources needed to perform joint administration of the LIHTC program is feasible and could be based on HUD's experience administering other housing programs. Having an estimate on potential costs and funding options for financing federal oversight of the LIHTC program will help HUD and congressional decision makers in assessing potential changes to the administration of the program.

CONCLUSIONS

Although LIHTC is the largest federal program for increasing the supply of affordable rental housing, LIHTC is a peripheral program in IRS in terms of resources and mission. Oversight responsibilities for the program include monitoring HFAs and taxpayer compliance. However, IRS oversight of HFAs has been minimal, particularly in reviewing QAPs and conducting audits of HFAs. Without regular monitoring of HFAs, IRS is not able to determine the extent to which HFAs comply with program requirements. Despite the importance of the program in the affordable rental housing market, program managers and congressional decision makers do not have sufficient information to assess the program's effectiveness.

Significant resource constraints have affected IRS's ability to oversee taxpayer compliance and currently preclude wide-ranging improvement to such functions, but IRS still has an opportunity to enhance oversight of taxpayer compliance in the LIHTC program. Reliable data on credit allocations and certifications would enable IRS to assess basic compliance requirements. IRS has acknowledged the need for improvements in its controls and procedures (including data entry and quality reviews). Federal internal control standards state effective information technology management is critical to achieving useful, reliable, and continuous recording and communication of information. IRS officials agreed that these problems should be corrected and data quality reviews be conducted on an ongoing basis.

Moreover, leveraging the experience and expertise of another agency with a housing mission, such as HUD, may help offset some of IRS's limitations in relation to program oversight. Unlike the jointly administered Historic Rehabilitation and New Markets tax credit programs, IRS is the sole federal administrator in LIHTC and HUD has a limited role in the program. Expanding HUD's role—making it a joint program administrator—could enhance LIHTC oversight. Although we and others have identified weakness in HUD's evaluation and oversight of programs, HUD already has processes and procedures in place for evaluation and oversight of state and local agencies—they constitute a framework on which further changes and improvements in LIHTC could be effected. Under joint administration, IRS could continue to retain certain key responsibilities consistent with its tax administration mission. But assigning oversight responsibilities to HUD (such as reviewing QAPs, developing goals and performance measures, and collecting LIHTC data) could involve additional staff and other resources. The other tax credit programs we reviewed illustrate some of the different funding mechanisms such as fees that might be used to help fund new oversight for LIHTC. An estimate of potential costs and funding options for financing enhanced federal oversight of the LIHTC program would be integral to determining an appropriate funding mechanism.

Matter for Congressional Consideration

To better align program goals with agency missions and improve program administration and oversight, Congress should consider designating the Department of Housing and Urban Development as a joint administrator of the program responsible for oversight.

As part of the deliberation, Congress also should direct HUD to estimate the costs to monitor and perform the additional oversight responsibilities, including a discussion of funding options.

Recommendation for Executive Action

To improve the utility of the credit allocation information contained in IRS's database, IRS should address weaknesses identified in data entry and programming controls to ensure reliable data are collected.

Agency and Third-Party Comments and Our Evaluation

We provided a draft of this report to HUD, Interior, IRS, and Treasury for their review and comment. IRS, Treasury, and HUD provided written comments. IRS and Treasury also provided technical comments that were incorporated, as appropriate. Interior did not provide any comments on the draft report. We also provided a draft to the National Council of State Housing Agencies (NCSHA), a nonprofit organization that represents the HFAs, for its review and comment.

IRS agreed with our recommendation that it should address weaknesses in data entry and programming controls to ensure reliable data are collected. IRS noted that reliable data would enable it to more effectively assess basic compliance requirements. According to IRS's comments, significant resource constraints have affected IRS's ability to improve its database and implement other improvements in its procedures and controls. Additionally IRS noted that its review of hundreds of audits found no widespread compliance issues and therefore the agency performed no ongoing tracking of audit results and trends. However, as our report notes, IRS conducted this analysis in 2000 for a sample of 402 audits of LIHTC taxpayers performed from 1995 through 1999 and had not updated this review for nearly 15 years. Federal internal control standards state that monitoring should occur in the course of normal operations, be performed continually, and be ingrained in the agency's operations. As a result, the agency does not have current knowledge of the level of noncompliance or if more monitoring were needed. IRS noted that it expects to take action in response to our recommendation to improve the utility of the credit allocation information contained in its database and improve monitoring. IRS did not comment on the matter for congressional consideration (to designate HUD as a joint administrator of the program responsible for oversight).

Treasury agreed that it would be useful for HUD to receive ongoing responsibility for, and resources to perform, research and analysis on the effectiveness of LIHTCs in increasing the availability of affordable rental housing. Treasury noted that such research and analysis is not part of IRS's responsibilities or consistent with its expertise in interpreting and enforcing tax laws. However, Treasury stated that responsibility for interpreting and enforcing the code should remain entirely with IRS. Similarly, our report notes that under joint administration, IRS could retain certain key responsibilities consistent with its tax administration mission. In considering the utility of HUD's expanded role in LIHTC, Treasury noted that research and analysis by HUD might help address whether HFAs' allocations of LIHTCs affirmatively addressed fair housing concerns and whether the allocations have been effective in meeting other congressional goals. Treasury further observed that if HUD's research and analysis indicated a need for additional interpretation or guidance, then Treasury and IRS could improve guidance or change the approach to enforcement. Coordinating on findings from any analyses conducted by HUD would be a positive step towards strengthening oversight of the program. As our report notes, IRS has performed minimal oversight of HFAs, particularly in terms of analyzing QAPs and conducting on-site or desk audits of HFAs. Thus, leveraging the experience and expertise of another agency with a housing mission may help offset some of IRS's limitations in relation to program oversight. HUD could assume certain oversight responsibilities, such as reviewing QAPs of HFAs, monitoring of HFAs' compliance with key responsibilities, identifying goals and performance measures, and collecting more programwide data.

HUD did not expressly comment on the matter for congressional consideration (to designate HUD as a joint administrator of the LIHTC program responsible for oversight). However, it supported consideration of a structure for enhanced interagency coordination on housing policy, including the LIHTC program. HUD noted that such a structure could help ensure the program's alignment with federal housing goals, such as creating affordable housing in areas of high opportunity and fueling reinvestment in high-poverty communities. HUD has conducted dedicated research on LIHTC; for example, on the effect of incentives in state QAPs on the location of LIHTC properties. However, HUD noted that Congress would need to appropriate additional resources to any agency assigned the responsibility to provide oversight, review QAPs, and conduct further in-depth research on LIHTC. HUD stated that it did not receive any appropriations authorized for its collection of LIHTC tenant data, which delayed HUD's ability to publicly release data. Our report also notes that assigning programmatic oversight responsibilities for LIHTC to another agency could require additional staff and other resources. We examined other tax credit programs with joint administration and found that each used varying mechanisms to fund its activities, including user fees and appropriations, which could serve as examples of how an agency may fund new oversight of LIHTCs.

NCSHA disagreed with our matter for congressional consideration. NCSHA stated that if Congress believed more oversight was needed, NCSHA would prefer to see Congress place those resources within Treasury and IRS to build on the program expertise in those agencies, partly because it asserted that HUD has "virtually no experience" with the LIHTC program. NCSHA noted that state HFAs have worked closely with Treasury and IRS to ensure proper administration of the program. Our report recognizes the various ways that IRS officials work with state HFAs to implement the program, but it also notes significant oversight deficiencies in IRS's administration of the program. Our report also highlights several reasons why HUD may be an appropriate agency to jointly administer certain aspects of the LIHTC program. First, HUD is the federal government's lead housing agency, and as such, has responsibilities for reporting on federal efforts to meet the nation's affordable housing and fair housing goals. Second, HUD has experience working with HFAs on various programs, including its rental assistance programs, and through its risk-sharing agreements with HFAs. LIHTC projects also may be recipients of funds from other federal programs, including HUD-administered programs such as HOME and project-based Section 8 rental assistance. Third, HUD has a framework (processes, procedures, and staff) in place for program evaluation and oversight of state and local agencies that could be expanded and strengthened. Finally, HUD already has a data collection role in the LIHTC program. While this role is limited to mandatory data collection on tenant characteristics, such as race and income, and voluntarily maintaining data on LIHTC properties, a joint oversight role could allow HUD to directly collect nationwide data on LIHTC properties needed to assess program effectiveness. Whereas currently, statutory restrictions prevent the disclosure of taxpayer information collected by IRS to HUD. As a result, we maintain HUD, an agency with a housing mission and whose current programs regularly interact with the LIHTC program, is in a better position to perform some oversight functions for LIHTC. Also, in commenting on this report, Treasury recognized that it would be useful to have HUD receive ongoing responsibility for research and analysis on the effectiveness of LIHTCs.

NCSHA also questioned if it was fair of GAO to judge Treasury and IRS oversight by the amount of data collected or number of audits conducted and with seemingly little attention to the program's successful housing results. In the report, we cite that monitoring should occur in the course of normal operations, be performed continually, and be ingrained in the agency's operations. IRS does not regularly review QAPs or conduct on- site reviews of HFAs. More specifically, IRS had conducted only seven audits of HFAs since the program's inception in 1986. IRS officials stated the lack in oversight was caused by a lack of resources and competing demands. Furthermore, we note that activities need to be established to monitor performance measures and indicators, which includes comparing data so that analyses can be conducted. However, we found that IRS has not set goals or assessed performance for the program, collected limited data needed to administer and enforce the tax code, and the data it collected are not reliable. The LIHTC program is the largest source of federal assistance for developing affordable rental housing and cost an estimated $8 billion in forgone revenue in 2014. Therefore, it is critical that program managers and congressional decision makers have reliable data available to judge the effectiveness and level of compliance of the program.

NCSHA also stated that joint administration of the LIHTC program would create additional red tape (a new level of bureaucracy) and could result in reduced program effectiveness and housing production. Our review focused on IRS's oversight functions, including monitoring taxpayers and state HFAs and reviewing program data for program effectiveness and compliance. We did not suggest a comprehensive change to how IRS administers LIHTC. Rather, we recommend an approach to provide Congress and taxpayers with a greater understanding of how the program operates and performs. In our review of other tax credit programs (similar in purpose and structure to LIHTC) that were jointly administered by IRS and other federal agencies, we found the other federal agencies provided key oversight and administrative support, such as monitoring, performance measurement, and data collection. Under joint administration with HUD, IRS, with its tax expertise, could continue to retain certain key responsibilities in implementing the program in partnership with state HFAs. Joint administration of the program will involve dividing responsibilities for one program across two agencies, and our expectation would be that IRS and HUD will carefully define their respective roles and responsibilities and have clear lines of communication to help ensure the program does not create any unnecessary inefficiencies, such as duplicative or overlapping requirements for HFAs. In addition, Congress can define specific requirements and limits of each agency's oversight responsibilities.

Finally, NCSHA noted that HFAs have a track record of outstanding performance in affordable housing finance and that Congress and the Administration entrusted HFAs to administer federal housing programs. In addition, NCSHA stated GAO had positively recognized HFAs for the LIHTC program in past reports. We acknowledged in our report that the LIHTC program was the largest federal program for increasing the supply of affordable rental housing and the design of the program can result in HFAs and other entities, including investors and syndicators, providing project oversight. We also made these points in prior work. But we also noted in prior work dating to 1997 that procedures for reviewing QAPs and monitoring compliance could be improved, and that LIHTC data were not sufficient to measure program success. Joint administration with an agency with a housing mission could help offset these longstanding deficiencies in IRS's oversight of the program.

Sincerely yours,
Daniel Garcia-Diaz
Director, Financial Markets
and Community Investment

APPENDIX I: OBJECTIVES, SCOPE, AND METHODOLOGY

This report discusses the Low-Income Housing Tax Credit (LIHTC) program, which is administered by the Internal Revenue Service (IRS) and state housing finance agencies (HFA). More specifically, this report (1) discusses how the LIHTC program is administered; (2) evaluates processes for overseeing the LIHTC program; and (3) compares the administration of other tax credit programs with LIHTC.

To determine how the LIHTC program is administered, we reviewed IRS regulations and guidance that describe IRS's roles and responsibilities in administering the LIHTC program, including overseeing HFAs and taxpayers. We also reviewed documentation on the role of HFAs, investors, and syndicators in the program.[70] Because LIHTC projects are often financed with funds from other programs, we reviewed the monitoring requirements for some federal programs present in LIHTC projects, such as the HOME Investment Partnerships (HOME) program and project-based Section 8. To illustrate the number of LIHTC projects containing other federal funding, we also reviewed a publication issued by the National Council of State Housing Agencies (NCSHA) on survey results.[71] We assessed the reliability of these data by interviewing NCSHA officials and reviewing documentation on survey techniques used to collect the data. We determined the data were reliable for our purposes of reporting on other funding sources for LIHTC projects. We interviewed officials from IRS, the Department of the Treasury (Treasury), Department of Housing and Urban Development (HUD), selected HFAs, and NCSHA on the administration of the program. We also conducted interviews at the Georgia HFA and Illinois HFA to help provide examples of how the programs were administered at the state level. We selected these two HFAs based on prior work conducted at these locations for other GAO reports on the Tax Credit Assistance Program (TCAP), administered by HUD, and the Grants to States for Low-Income Housing Projects in Lieu of Low-Income Housing Credits (Section 1602) program, administered by Treasury. Our prior work is relevant because it assessed HFA administration and oversight of these programs and because we discuss TCAP and 1602 in this report. We also selected these sites because of their proximity to GAO locations. Moreover, we interviewed a certified public accounting and consulting firm, Novogradac & Company LLP. We selected this firm because of its role in the LIHTC working group—a forum for participants in the LIHTC program to work together to resolve technical and administrative issues relating to the LIHTC program—and because of the information on the firm's website on HFAs and guidance for the LIHTC program.

To evaluate processes for overseeing the LIHTC program, we reviewed applicable forms and guidance used to monitor the program, and reviewed IRS audits of HFAs conducted from 2003 to 2014 to determine the frequency with which audits were conducted and the types of findings identified.[72] We reviewed IRS's process for identifying and conducting audits on taxpayers claiming LIHTCs from 2001 to 2013 and how the results of these audits were used to inform management about the types of noncompliance and to track the effectiveness of program monitoring. We reviewed federal internal control standards to identify key activities that help ensure that a program addresses requirements and appropriate actions are taken to address program risks.[73] We also reviewed the strategic and annual reports of IRS, Treasury, and HUD to determine the program goals and outcome information available for the LIHTC program. We analyzed information contained in IRS's Low-Income Housing Credit database from December 2005 to August 2014. Specifically, we reviewed available information from forms on the credit allocation and certification (form 8609) and the noncompliance or building disposition (form 8823).[74] We assessed the reliability of the database by reviewing documentation, performing electronic testing, and interviewing the relevant officials responsible for administering and overseeing the database. We also conducted reasonableness checks on the data to identify any missing, erroneous, or outlying figures. We determined we would not be able to rely on the data to perform our analysis. Therefore, we limited our discussion of the database to the type of information collected, the extent to which the information was collected, and potential analysis that could be conducted if the data were more complete and accurate. We also reviewed an IRS staff proposal for statutory changes to allow IRS to disclose certain protected information so that HUD could help assess the completeness of the data it received on LIHTC tenant characteristics and reviewed a prior GAO report that discussed statutory exceptions related to data sharing of confidential taxpayer information.[75] Lastly, we interviewed IRS and selected HFA officials about monitoring procedures for the LIHTC program and Treasury and HUD officials on program goals and outcomes and statutory barriers that may prevent information sharing for the LIHTC program.

To compare the administration of other tax credit programs with LIHTC, we reviewed tax credit programs administered by IRS to identify those that are most similar in purpose and structure to LIHTC. We focused on the Historic Rehabilitation Tax Credit and New Markets Tax Credit programs because, similar to the LIHTC program, both are aimed at encouraging community development and each is jointly administered by IRS and another federal entity—the Department of Interior's National Park Service (NPS) and Treasury's Community Development Financial Institutions (CDFI) Fund, respectively.[76] In addition to administrative structures, our review focused on how these two programs conducted monitoring, used performance measures, and collected data. We reviewed prior GAO reports related to each of these programs.[77] Moreover, we reviewed HUD's role in working with state and local agencies and its role in the LIHTC program. We also reviewed information available in the *State HFA Factbook: NCSHA 2012 Annual Survey Results* to gain an understanding of how HFAs use fees to administer the LIHTC program. We assessed the reliability of these data by interviewing NCSHA officials and reviewing documentation on survey techniques used to collect the data. We determined the data were reliable for our purposes of reviewing how HFAs use fees to administer the LIHTC program. Additionally, we interviewed officials from the Departments of Interior and Treasury and the CDFI Fund concerning the administration of the Historic Rehabilitation Tax Credit and New Markets Tax Credit programs and how the programs funded administrative costs. We met with IRS officials to discuss their role in the administration of the Historic Rehabilitation Tax Credit.

We conducted this performance audit from February 2014 through July 2015 in accordance with generally accepted government auditing standards. Those standards require that we plan and perform the audit to obtain sufficient, appropriate evidence to provide a reasonable basis for our findings and conclusions based on our audit objectives. We believe that the evidence obtained provides a reasonable basis for our findings and conclusions based on our audit objectives.

End Notes

[1] We use "annual allocation of LIHTCs" in lieu of the statutory term, "state housing credit ceiling." The state housing credit ceiling is the aggregate amount of housing credit allocations that may be made in any calendar year by HFAs in the state and may not exceed the state's housing credit ceiling for such calendar year. The housing credit ceiling for each state for calendar year 2015 is the greater of $2.30 multiplied by the state's population or $2,680,000. A state's population for any calendar year is determined by reference to the most recent census estimate (whether final or provisional) released by the Bureau of the Census before the beginning of the calendar year for which the housing credit ceiling is set.

[2] We use "LIHTC" or "tax credits" rather than the statutory term, "housing credit dollar amount," which is defined as an HFA's apportionment of the state housing credit ceiling for such year.

[3] Senate Committee on Appropriations, Subcommittee on Financial Services and General Government, *Review of the President's Fiscal Year 2016 Funding Request for the Department of the Treasury and the Internal Revenue Service*, 114th Cong., 1st sess., March 3, 2015; testimony of J. Russell George, Treasury Inspector General for Tax Administration. For the same hearing, also see testimony of Nina E. Olson, National Taxpayer Advocate.

[4] GAO, *Internal Revenue Service Observations on IRS's Operations, Planning, and Resources,* GAO-15-420R (Washington, D.C.: Feb. 27, 2015).

[5] Syndicators are intermediaries that connect developers seeking equity investments in an LIHTC project with investors and charge a fee for overseeing the investment transaction. HOME is administered by HUD, and provides formula grants to localities and states to fund activities that build, buy, or rehabilitate affordable housing for rent or homeownership or provide direct rental assistance to low-income people. HUD's project-based Section 8 rental assistance program provides rental subsidies for eligible tenant families. All such assistance is project-based, meaning that HUD commits the subsidy for the assisted units of a particular property for a contractually determined period.

[6] We conducted interviews at the Georgia HFA and Illinois HFA to determine how the program was administered. We selected these two HFAs based on prior work conducted at these locations for other GAO reports on the Tax Credit Assistance Program (TCAP) administered by HUD, and the Grants to States for Low-Income Housing Projects in Lieu of Low-Income Housing Credits (Section 1602) program administered by Treasury. Our prior work is relevant because it assessed HFA administration and oversight of these programs and because we discuss TCAP and 1602 in this report. We also selected these sites because of their proximity to GAO locations. We have additional work under way on HFAs.

[7] IRS began conducting HFA audits in 2003. We reviewed audits of HFAs conducted from 2003 to 2014.

[8] GAO, *Standards for Internal Control in the Federal Government,* GAO/ AIMD-00-21.3.1 (Washington, D.C.: November 1999).

[9] For information on community development tax expenditures, including the Historic Rehabilitation and New Markets tax credits, we reviewed GAO, *Community Development: Limited Information on the Use and Effectiveness of Tax Expenditures Could Be Mitigated through Congressional Attention*, GAO-12-262 (Washington, D.C.: Feb. 29, 2012). For the Historic Rehabilitation Tax Credit, we reviewed GAO, *Information on Historic Preservation Tax Incentives*, GAO/ GGD-84-47 (Washington, D.C.: Mar. 29, 1984); and *Tax Policy and Administration: Historic Preservation Tax Incentives*, GGD-86-112FS (Washington, D.C.: Aug. 1, 1986). For the New Markets Tax Credit, we reviewed GAO, *New Markets Tax Credit Program: Progress Made in Implementation, but Further Actions Needed to Monitor Compliance*, GAO-04-326 (Washington, D.C.: Jan. 30, 2004);*Tax Policy: New Markets Tax Credit Appears to Increase Investment by Investors in Low-Income Communities, but Opportunities Exist to Better Monitor Compliance*, GAO-07-296 (Washington, D.C.: Jan.

31, 2007); *New Markets Tax Credit: The Credit Helps Fund a Variety of Projects in Low-Income Communities, but Could Be Simplified*, GAO-10-334 (Washington, D.C.: Jan. 29, 2010); *Community Development Financial Institutions and New Markets Tax Credit Programs in Metropolitan and Nonmetropolitan Areas*, GAO-12-547R (Washington, D.C.: Apr. 26, 2012); and *New Markets Tax Credit: Better Controls and Data Are Needed to Ensure Effectiveness*, GAO-14-500 (Washington, D.C.: July 10, 2014).

[10] 26 USC §§ 42(h)(3),(m).

[11] Projects are considered placed in service on the date on which the first unit in the building is ready and available for occupancy under state or local law. The amount of credit the taxpayer can claim each year is determined by the following calculations: (1) eligible basis x applicable fraction = qualified basis; and (2) qualified basis x applicable percentage = annual credit amount. The eligible basis is the total allowable costs associated with depreciable costs in the residential rental project. The applicable fraction is the portion of rental units that are qualified low-income units in relation to total residential rental units. The applicable percentage is the discount factor needed to limit the annual credit to the present value of either 70 or 30 percent of the qualified basis, depending on the characteristics of the housing.

[12] HFAs and the taxpayers enter into an extended use agreement at the start of the credit period.

[13] In 2008, with the passage of the Housing and Economic Recovery Act, HFAs were required to submit annual data to HUD on race, ethnicity, family composition, age, income, use of rental assistance under Section 8(o) of the United States Housing Act of 1937 or other similar assistance, disability status, and monthly rental payments of households residing in each property receiving Low-Income Housing Tax Credits. HUD also was required to make the data it receives available to the public and does so through the LIHTC databases (http://lihtc.huduser.org/).

[14] A difficult development area is defined as "any area designated by the Secretary of HUD as an area which has high construction, land, and utility costs relative to area median gross income." 26 U.S.C § 42(d)(5)(B)(iii)(I). HUD updates the list of such areas annually. For example, see, 79 Fed. Reg. 59854 (Oct. 3, 2014). Qualified census tracts are designated by the Secretary of HUD and include tracts in which either 50 percent or more of households have income below 60 percent of the area median gross income or the poverty rate is at least 25 percent. 26 U.S.C § 42(d)(5)(B)(ii)(I).

[15] The QAP describes the HFA's compliance with Section 42 requirements. For instance, it should show that the HFA gave preference to projects that serve the tenants with the lowest incomes, serve qualifying tenants for the longest period of time, and are located in a qualified census tract and the development of which contributes to a concerted community revitalization plan.

[16] We will issue a subsequent report on the role of syndicators and the costs of the LIHTC program.

[17] IRS's Large Business and International Division assigned one analyst to perform part- time functions in the LIHTC program, as needed.

[18] Compliance unit staff assist other IRS units and the 5.6 full-time equivalents do not necessarily spend all their time on LIHTC tasks. A full-time equivalent is a measure of staff hours equal to those of an employee who works 2,080 hours per year, or 40 hours per week for 52 weeks.

[19] The audit technique guide for form 8823 was last updated in January 2011. According to IRS officials, the first Low-Income Housing Credit Audit Technique Guide was introduced in 1999. IRS released updated guidance in 2014 to internal and external stakeholders. See *Audit Technique Guide, IRC §42, Low-Income Housing Credit* (Rev. 09-2014) and *Audit Technique Guide, Guide for Completing Form 8823, Low-Income Housing Credit Agencies Report of Noncompliance or Building Disposition* (Rev. 01-2011).

[20] The term "state" includes a possession of the United States. 26 U.S.C 42(h)(8). All 50 states, the District of Columbia, and five U.S. possessions (American Samoa, Guam, the Northern

Mariana Islands, Puerto Rico, and the U.S. Virgin Islands) have HFAs that receive LIHTC allocations.

[21] HOME is administered by HUD, and provides formula grants to localities and states to fund activities that build, buy, or rehabilitate affordable housing for rent or homeownership or provide direct rental assistance to low-income people. HUD's project-based Section 8 rental assistance program provides rental subsidies for eligible tenant families.

[22] National Council of State Housing Agencies, *State HFA Factbook: 2012 NCSHA Annual Survey Results* (Washington, D.C.: 2014). Not all 54 HFAs surveyed responded to all questions. We determined the data were reliable for the purpose of reporting on other funding sources for LIHTC projects. More specifically, 47 of 51 HFAs responded that a percentage of LIHTC units received HOME funds and 36 of 50 HFAs said a percentage of LIHTC units received project-based Section 8 funds. Projects also may include funds from the Community Development Block Grant (CDBG) program (an average of 3 percent of units received these funds); Department of Agriculture's Multifamily Direct Rural Rental Housing loans—Section 515 (an average of 5.6 percent of units received these funds); and Historic Rehabilitation Tax Credit (an average of 3.6 percent of units received these funds).

[23] HUD pays performance-based contract administrators an incentive fee if they performed above a minimum quality level as determined by HUD or reduces their fee if they performed below it.

[24] Statutory authorities include the Fair Housing Act, Title VI of the Civil Rights Act of 1964, Section 109 of Title I of the Housing and Community Development Act of 1974, Section 504 of the Rehabilitation Act of 1973, and Title II of the Americans with Disabilities Act.

[25] Price in LIHTCs refers to the amount an investor is willing to pay for the credit.

[26] Asset management includes the many activities that relate to monitoring and planning for the long-term financial and physical health and viability of a project. For example, asset-management activities examine plans for addressing a project's capital needs, changes in market conditions, and recommendations and implementation of plans to correct troubled projects. Asset managers are likely to take a much closer look at a project's finances than HFAs would for long-term compliance monitoring. We previously recommended that Treasury assess the extent to which HFAs utilize information provided to them by project owners to ensure the long-term viability of buildings during the 15-year compliance period. GAO, *Recovery Act: Housing Programs Met Spending Milestones, but Asset Management Information Needs Evaluation*, GAO-12-634 (Washington, D.C.: June 18, 2012).

[27] Congress enacted the Single Audit Act, 31 U.S.C. §§ 7501-7507, in 1984 for purposes that include promoting sound financial management for federal awards administered by nonfederal entities. The act requires states, local governments, and nonprofits expending $750,000 or more in federal awards in a year to obtain an audit in accordance with the requirements in the act. A single audit includes an audit and opinions on the fair presentation of the financial statements and testing of internal control over financial reporting and the entity's compliance with program requirements.

[28] GAO/AIMD-00-21.3.1.

[29] We have been conducting an in-depth review of HFA QAPs for a forthcoming report on HFA oversight of LIHTC projects.

[30] 26 U.S.C. 42(m)(1)(A)-(C). In housing grant programs, such as HOME, HUD staff review consolidated plans before grant funds are awarded.

[31] Internal Revenue Service, Chief Counsel Advice Memorandum 200913013 (Washington, D.C.: Mar. 27, 2009). Section 42(m)(1)(A)(i) provides that the housing credit for any building shall be zero unless the credit was allocated pursuant to a qualified allocation plan. One of the requirements for a qualified allocation plan under Section 42(m)(1)(B)(iii) is that the agency must monitor for compliance with the requirements of Section 42.

[32] IRS categorizes the audits of the state HFAs as containing taxpayer protected data under Section 6103 of the Internal Revenue Code. As such, we are omitting the state names and audit details. Federal tax information is kept confidential under Section 6103, except as

specifically authorized by law. Information in a form that cannot be associated with or otherwise identify, directly or indirectly, a particular taxpayer is not federal tax information. Section 6103 specifies what federal tax information can be disclosed, to whom, and for what purpose. In general, federal tax information is collected and developed to administer tax law. However, this information can be useful for other purposes, such as to detect possible noncompliance with nontax criminal laws or administer other kinds of programs.

[33] IRS began audits of HFAs in 2003.

[34] GAO, *Tax Credits: Opportunities to Improve Oversight of the Low-Income Housing Program*, GAO/GGD/RCED-97-55 (Washington, D.C.: Mar. 28, 1997).

[35] In 1995, IRS instituted an audit program (including training, development of an audit technique guide, and results reporting) to determine whether taxpayers were entitled to the credits claimed on their returns. From 1995 to 1997, audits were selected based on HFA responses on the noncompliance or building disposition form (8823). The case selection process was changed in January 1997 to include a broader range of taxpayers claiming the credit that were identified based on the credit allocation and certification form (8609) and filed tax returns.

[36] The audit results were unknown for the remaining audits, generally older audits, due to data not being collected or recorded.

[37] GAO, *Single Audit: Actions Needed to Ensure That Findings Are Corrected*, GAO-02-705 (Washington, D.C.: June 26, 2002).

[38] GAO, *High-Risk Series: An Update*, GAO-15-290 (Washington, D.C.: Feb. 11, 2015).

[39] GAO/AIMD-00-21.3.1.

[40] GAO, *Opportunities to Reduce Potential Duplication in Government Programs, Save Tax Dollars, and Enhance Revenue*, GAO-11-318SP (Washington, D.C.: Mar. 1, 2011).

[41] Data were missing for three main reasons: (1) inconsistent reporting by HFAs; (2) lack of follow up by HUD with HFAs when data were inconsistent from previous years; and (3) delays because of timing (of when HFAs receive data). See GAO, *Low-Income Housing Tax Credits: Agencies Implemented Changes Enacted in 2008, but Project Data Collection Could Be Improved*, GAO-13-66 (Washington, D.C.: Dec. 6, 2012).

[42] See Department of Housing and Urban Development, Office of Policy Development and Research, *Understanding Whom the LIHTC Program Serves: Tenants in LIHTC Units as of December 31, 2012*; accessed at http://www.huduser.org/portal/elist/2015-jan_20.html.

[43] Tax expenditures are reductions in a taxpayer's tax liability that result from special credits; deductions, exemptions, and exclusions from taxation; deferral of tax liability; and preferential tax rates. See Office of Management and Budget, *Preparation, Submission, and Execution of the Budget, Part 6, Strategic Plans, Annual Performance Plans, Performance Reviews, and Annual Program Performance Reports*, Circular No. A-11 (Washington, D.C.: July 2014, revised November 2014).

[44] Department of Housing and Urban Development, *FY 2013 Annual Performance Report and FY 2015 Annual Performance Plan* (Washington, D.C.: July 2014).

[45] GAO, *Performance Measurement and Evaluation: Definitions and Relationships*, GAO-11-646SP (Washington, D.C.: May 2011).

[46] The database was upgraded in November 2008, after it was taken offline in 2005 due to issues with the database program. Data from 1986 to 2005 were incorporated in the database when it was upgraded.

[47] We received records contained in IRS's Low-Income Housing Credit database from December 2005 to August 2014.

[48] GAO/AIMD-00-21.3.1.

[49] Federal tax information is kept confidential under Section 6103 of the Internal Revenue Code, except as specifically authorized by law.

[50] HUD's LIHTC databases are the federal government's main source of information on LIHTC projects. With the passage of the Housing and Economic Recovery Act of 2008, HUD was

required to collect data on tenant characteristics, such as race and income. Pub. L. No. 110-289 § 2835(d). 122 Stat. 2874 (2008).

[51] See GAO, *Taxpayer Privacy: A Guide for Screening and Assessing Proposals to Disclose Confidential Tax Information to Specific Parties for Specific Purposes*, GAO-12-231SP (Washington, D.C.: Dec. 14, 2011).

[52] For the Historic Rehabilitation Tax Credit program, we focused on the 20 percent tax credit for rehabilitating certified historic structures and did not include other tax credits (such as the 10 percent rehabilitation tax credit for nonhistoric structures) or tax deductions associated with donations of historic preservation easements. We selected the two programs in part because they shared several features with LIHTC: (1) the tax credits reduce a taxpayer's federal tax liability as a result of that taxpayer's investment in certain qualified assets or projects; (2) tax credits are awarded on the basis of a federal or state entity's prior review, approval, or certification; and (3) these programs do not include other tax incentives, such as deductions and exemptions. For more information on our methodology, see appendix I.

[53] We did not audit the data collection processes for the Historic Rehabilitation Tax Credit or assess the completeness or accuracy of the data collected for the program

[54] We did not audit the oversight functions of the Historic Rehabilitation Tax Credit or New Markets Tax Credit, but note that each program has resources devoted to oversight.

[55] Department of the Interior, National Park Service, Technical Preservation Services, *Federal Tax Incentives for Rehabilitating Historic Buildings: Annual Report for Fiscal Year 2014* (Washington, D.C.: March 2015); and *Federal Tax Incentives for Rehabilitating Historic Buildings: Statistical Report and Analysis for Fiscal Year 2014* (Washington, D.C.: March 2015).

[56] For a recent version of this report, see Department of the Interior, National Park Service, Technical Preservation Services, *Annual Report on the Economic Impact of the Federal Historic Tax Credit for FY 2013* (Washington, D.C.: August 2014).

[57] We did not audit the data collection processes of the Historic Rehabilitation Tax Credit or assess the completeness or accuracy of the data collected for the program.

[58] Martin D. Abravanel, et al., *New Markets Tax Credit (NMTC) Program Evaluation Final Report*, a report prepared for the Community Development Financial Institutions Fund (Washington, D.C.: April 2013).

[59] The federal government provides assistance for financing rental housing through 25 programs, tax expenditures, and other tools administered by four federal agencies; see GAO, *Housing Assistance: Opportunities Exist to Increase Collaboration and Consider Consolidation*, GAO-12-554 (Washington, D.C.: Aug. 16, 2012); and *2012 Annual Report: Opportunities to Reduce Duplication, Overlap and Fragmentation, Achieve Savings, and Enhance Revenue*, GAO-12-342SP (Washington, D.C.: Feb. 28, 2012).

[60] Department of Housing and Urban Development, *FY 2013 Annual Performance Report, and FY 2015 Annual Performance Plan* (Washington, D.C.: July 2014).

[61] The CDBG program (begun in 1974) provides annual grants on a formula basis to local governments and states.

[62] Participating qualified state and local HFAs may originate and underwrite affordable housing loans, including new construction, substantial rehabilitation, refinancing, and housing for the elderly. The program provides mortgage insurance (by the Federal Housing Administration) to enhance HFA bonds to investment-grade. HFAs may elect to share 10–90 percent of the loss on a loan with HUD. The HFA reimburses HUD in the event of a claim pursuant to terms of the risk-sharing agreement.

[63] GAO-12-262.

[64] GAO, letter to congressional committees identifying GAO's original high-risk areas (Jan. 23, 1990).

[65] GAO-15-290.

[66] The Housing and Economic Recovery Act of 2008 authorized $6.1 million for fiscal years 2009 through 2013 for HUD, for purposes that included providing technical assistance to HFAs

and compiling the tenant data. But HUD never received any appropriations for these tasks. See GAO-13-66.

[67] According to TPS officials, the Historic Rehabilitation Tax Credit program is expected to support a $3.2 million budget in fiscal year 2015 based entirely on fees. We did not assess the use of user fees in the program.

[68] Rather than set fees, three HFAs charged a percentage of the credit. See National Council of State Housing Agencies, *State HFA Factbook: 2012 NCSHA Annual Survey Results* (Washington, D.C.: 2014).

[69] We have work under way reviewing other aspects of the LIHTC program, including HFA oversight, the role of syndicators in developing LIHTC projects, and the costs of developing projects.

[70] Syndicators are intermediaries that connect developers seeking equity investments in a LIHTC project with investors and charge a fee for overseeing the investment transaction.

[71] National Council of State Housing Agencies, *State HFA Factbook: 2012 NCSHA Annual Survey Results* (Washington, D.C.: 2014). We chose this group because it represents HFAs and advocates for affordable housing.

[72] IRS began conducting HFA audits in 2003, which determined our date range. IRS categorizes the audits of the state HFAs as containing taxpayer protected data under Section 6103 of the Internal Revenue Code. As such, we are omitting the state names and audit details. Federal tax information is kept confidential under Section 6103, except as specifically authorized by law. Information in a form that cannot be associated with or otherwise identify, directly or indirectly, a particular taxpayer is not federal tax information. Section 6103 specifies what federal tax information can be disclosed, to whom, and for what purpose. In general, federal tax information is collected and developed to administer tax law. However, this information can be useful for other purposes, such as to detect possible noncompliance with nontax criminal laws or administer other kinds of programs.

[73] GAO, *Standards for Internal Control in the Federal Government,* GAO/AIMD-00-21.3.1 (Washington, D.C.: November 1999).

[74] IRS's Low-Income Housing Credit database did not contain information collected on the HFA annual reports (form 8610).

[75] GAO, *Taxpayer Privacy: A Guide for Screening and Assessing Proposals to Disclose Confidential Tax Information to Specific Parties for Specific Purposes*, GAO-12-231SP (Washington, D.C.: Dec. 14, 2011).

[76] For the Historic Rehabilitation Tax Credit program, our review focused on the 20 percent tax credit for rehabilitating certified historic structures and did not include other historic tax credits, such as the 10 percent rehabilitation tax credit for nonhistoric structures or tax deductions associated with donations of historic preservation easements. We selected the Historic Rehabilitation Tax Credit and New Markets Tax Credit programs in part because they shared several features with LIHTC:(1) The tax credits reduce a taxpayer's federal tax liability as a result of that taxpayer's investment in certain qualified assets or projects. (2) Tax credits under these programs are awarded on the basis of a federal or state entity's prior review, approval or certification. (3) These tax credit programs do not include other tax incentives, such as deductions and exemptions.

[77] For information on community development tax expenditures, including the Historic Rehabilitation Tax Credit and New Markets Tax Credit, we reviewed GAO, *Community Development: Limited Information on the Use and Effectiveness of Tax Expenditures Could Be Mitigated through Congressional Attention*, GAO-12-262 (Washington, D.C.: Feb. 29, 2012). For the Historic Rehabilitation Tax Credit, we reviewed GAO, *Information on Historic Preservation Tax Incentives*, GAO/ GGD-84-47 (Washington, D.C.: Mar. 29, 1984); and *Tax Policy and Administration: Historic Preservation Tax Incentives*, GGD-86-112FS (Washington, D.C.: Aug. 1, 1986). For the New Markets Tax Credit, we reviewed GAO, *New Markets Tax Credit Program: Progress Made in Implementation, but Further Actions Needed to Monitor Compliance*, GAO-04-326 (Washington, D.C.: Jan. 30, 2004);

Tax Policy: New Markets Tax Credit Appears to Increase Investment by Investors in Low-Income Communities, but Opportunities Exist to Better Monitor Compliance, GAO-07-296 (Washington, D.C.: Jan. 31, 2007); *New Markets Tax Credit: The Credit Helps Fund a Variety of Projects in Low-Income Communities, but Could Be Simplified*, GAO-10-334 (Washington, D.C.: Jan. 29, 2010); *Community Development Financial Institutions and New Markets Tax Credit Programs in Metropolitan and Nonmetropolitan Areas*, GAO-12-547R (Washington, D.C.: Apr. 26, 2012); and *New Markets Tax Credit: Better Controls and Data Are Needed to Ensure Effectiveness*, GAO-14-500 (Washington, D.C.: July 10, 2014).

INDEX

A

B

C

D

E

F

G

H

I

J

L

M

N

O

P

Q

R

S

T

U

V

W